Discover! America's
Great River Road
Wisconsin, Iowa, Minnesota, Illinois

by
Pat Middleton

Heritage Press

•

Route 1, Stoddard, WI 54658

Published by Heritage Press
Stoddard, WI 54658

ISBN 0-9620823-3-3
Library of Congress Catalogue Card Number: 88-82228

What others are saying about this best-selling Guide to Mississippi River lore and recreation. . .

"This book is must reading! Pat Middleton has done super writing and research. The book is impossible to lay down for the information it contains."

Orville Meyers, long-time host of Iowa's radio and television program, *"Along the Outdoor Trails."*

"You opened up a whole new world for me and I appreciate that."

Reader, Duluth

"A well-researched, comprehensive guide."
The Bloomsbury Review, Colorado

"A terrific guide for those who relish boating, fishing, or cruising on land along the Mississippi River."
Review, **Booklist** Magazine

"The resource for adventuring between Minneapolis-St. Paul and Galena, IL."
Review, Minneapolis

"I drove the Great River Road from St. Paul to St. Louis last August, with this book at my side. When we passed out of its perameters, we felt a sense of loss. I eagerly await the release of Volume 2, Dubuque to St. Louis."
Review, **St. Louis Post Dispatch**

"A great book for planning weekend drives."
Review, **Rochester Post-Bulletin**

"I loved your book and have two friends who simply must have it!"
Reader, Eau Claire

CONTENTS

CONTENTS

PREFACE

My husband and I are travelers. Over the course of five years, we lived in London, Bangkok, Sydney, and Aix-en-Provence, France. We snorkled over the Great Barrier Reef, photographed the sunrise on Ayers Rock, taxied up the Malay peninsula, sailed in Fiji. But it is the Upper Mississippi River Valley that calls us home, partly because we have found here a little bit of everything we've admired most in the world.

The history of this area is significant not only to residents, but to the nation. Indian settlement of the Upper Mississippi dates back thousands of years. European traders and explorers were active in the area at the same time New York was a struggling village. Spain, France, England, and America have all made major investments in the discovery and exploitation of its adjoining shores.

The parade of tiny settlements which cling to the river's edge offer ethnic diversity matched only by a whirlwind tour of Europe. Syttende Mai, *Rendezvous!*, Oktoberfest, and Bastille Day are authentic old-world celebrations, complete with traditional dress, drink, and foods.

The natural history of the valley is unique in the north. Though untouched by recent glacial advances, the valley has been scoured and formed by unthinkable volumes of meltwater and glacial debris.

I hope you find the guide useful and enlightening. I have visited every village and wayside. I have met, and share with you, the stories of many marvelous people. May it add to your enjoyment of the Upper Mississippi.

Acknowledgments

It's been said that writing can be lonely work -- and at times it is -- but an author does not bring a book to publication alone. I owe a great debt of gratitude to many people.

A special thanks to those who served as resources or generously read through manuscripts -- in particular Dorothy Overson, Denyse Olson-Dorff, Robert Fisher, Caroline Middleton, Margaret Larson, and Ellie Anderson.

Several others contributed to other aspects of the book. A sincere thank you to the Graphics Department at Western Wisconsin Technical College where I learned desk-top publishing. The cover photo of Lansing, IA, was taken by Bill and Derva Burke of Lansing. Hank Schneider of the Upper Mississippi River National Wildlife and Fish Refuge provided many of the photos. Historical societies and individuals contributed background information on the small towns. To those who listened patiently as I enthused or reworked ideas, and to others who helped in so many ways, *my grateful thanks*.

Finally, it is to Richard, my husband and long-time traveling partner, and our daughters, Lisa and Laura, that I dedicate this book. It is their patience, encouragement, and friendship that gives me wings.

No, this has not been a lonely work, but something more akin to a symphony.

P.M.

HOW TO USE THIS BOOK

The backbone of *DISCOVER! AMERICA'S GREAT RIVER ROAD* is the amenities survey and accompanying maps produced by the Mississippi River Regional Planning Commission in 1982. The survey collected details on all public river access points along the Great River Road, including boat ramps, fisherman parking, trails, and public parks. This Guide updates that data and includes private amenities of interest to the traveler such as campgrounds, lodging, marinas, and seasonal attractions along the Mississippi River in Wisconsin, Iowa, Minnesota and Galena, IL.

The detailed maps are based on county road maps produced by the Wisconsin Department of Transportation. Because they show quite well the less-traveled county and local roadways, these maps should also be useful to cyclists interested in getting off the beaten track.

The Great River Road is designated on maps and roadside markers by a green steamboat pilot's wheel. You will find all state *(STH)* and county *(CTH)* highways to be in excellent condition.

The Great River Road Parkway is a program of highway improvement along both sides of the Mississippi River, from Canada to the Gulf of Mexico. Federally funded scenic easements, roadside parks, scenic

overlooks, off-road parks and forests, points of historical interest and other river-oriented facilities have been developed along both sides of the river.

The route followed by the maps and commentary in this Guide commences at Prescott, WI, on *USH 10* and continues south, following a number of state and county highways, to DeSoto, WI, where the traveler has the option of continuing on the Wisconsin side or crossing into Iowa on *STH 82*.

The scenic Iowa route extends south through Harpers Ferry, the Effigy Mounds National Monument and into McGregor where it crosses the river again into Prairie du Chien, WI, and continues south to the historic cities of Galena, IL, and Dubuque, IA, the destination of the Guide. Those intending to travel south to north can adapt this guide by starting from the end of the book.

Chapters 2 -11 each feature one of the counties through which the Great River Road passes. In most cases, there will be heritage, natural history and recreational highlights noted in the introductory overview of the county. The detailed information on each river access, historical marker, park and village is then consecutively numbered by county to correspond with the small area map notations (e.g., TE-3 TREMPEALEAU LAKES.)

I have endeavored to provide information on Bed & Breakfast inns, historical, cultural, and natural history background on each of the villages, as well as sites of interest to the traveler. Some background topics are included in the Table of Contents under the heading of *Special Features.* I hope you will also enjoy the special 'up close and personal' type interview labeled *Insight* which includes reflections from various persons whose lives are closely entwined with the river.

Campers will find the bold-print notation {} which indicates that the campground accepts **overnight campers** at a **reduced fee of $3** or less to those travelers using the Guide. Generally this applies to travelers who arrive after 5 p.m., leave by 10 a.m., and do not hook up to utilities.

There are several points of interest along the Minnesota shore that are easily accessible by river bridges from the Wisconsin side. Red Wing, Wabasha, Winona and La Crescent, MN, are included as side trips from the Wisconsin side.

The beauty of the Great River Road lies in traveling slowly; stopping to absorb the view, visiting a fish market, chatting with locals at the cafe. It is our Rhine River, an Everglades of the north with a national treasure of eagles, wildlife, and migrating waterfowl. It is "Little Italy," Norwegian spoken in the street, and elegant paddlewheelers.

It is my hope that this book will cause you to pause for a moment to enjoy an area bounded by, nurtured by and challenged by a great river. For in the end — whether Indian, fur trader, adventurer, immigrant, visitor or farmer — we are all travelers. Only the bluffs and the river are here to stay.

*The **Pasque Flower** is found locally only on the isolated, grassy, goat prairies of the southwest facing bluffs. **Pasque** is the French word for Easter. The Pasque Flower is one of the very first wildflowers to bloom in the spring.*

The Great Seal

GEOLOGY, GEOGRAPHY, NATURAL RESOURCES OF THE UPPER MISSISSIPPI RIVER VALLEY

It was to the "inexhaustible" supplies of lumber in the pine woods of the North and the oak clad hills of the Mississippi River that the Upper Mississippi River Valley owes much of its development.

In the earliest days, French voyageurs shipped millions of dollars worth of luxurious furs out of the virgin forests via the Mississippi and the rivers of bordering states. The Mississippi has been a transportation corridor ever since. Daring entrepreneurs preceded the steamboats, stockpiling logs to be sold as fuel along the river banks. Then, after the Civil War, the Lumber Barons moved in, bringing with them shopkeepers, immigrant families, churches, and capital.

The railroads followed to transport logs and freight and to provide passenger service. They, too, followed the Mississippi Valley as the easiest route north. The hardwood forests provided fuel for steam engines and oak for constructing trestles and track. New immigrants found ready employment on section gangs maintaining the track.

The logging industry flourished for about ten years, from 1880-1890, accounting for nearly one-fourth of all wages paid in the state of Wisconsin during the logging days. Crews clearcut section after section, making no effort to replenish the resource as they moved through. Tree tops, scrub and young trees were decimated by uncontrolled forest fires.

Today, due to careful management by the Forestry Service, 45% of Wisconsin is again forested and productive. Northern forests that once supplied lumber for settlers in the treeless plains, now produce mainly fence posts and railroad ties and pulpwood for the paper industry.

Early Settlers

The native population of the Upper Mississippi is Indian. Indians were first discovered by the French explorer Jean Nicolet, who was sent to explore the lands west of the Great Lakes. Tribes believed to be in Wisconsin at this time included the Chippewa, Ottawa, Potawatomie, Menominee, and Winnebago. The Sac, Fox, Sioux and others moved into the area as they were displaced from homelands by the intrusion of the white man.

The first whites were French and Canadian fur traders and explorers. These adventurers fixed the sites of the first settlements and left many with French names (Dubuque, Pepin, La Crosse, Prairie du Chien, Trempealeau).

The French barely exists today as an ethnic group although the Upper Mississippi was a French territory until the end of the French and Indian Wars (1763). It was a British territory until the end of the War of 1812.

Two great population movements were significant in the settlement of the Upper Mississippi. The migrating lead miners organized the very first permanent settlements in Galena, Dubuque and Cassville in the 1820's and 30's and dominated the early history of the old Wisconsin Territory. Established in 1837, the Wisconsin Territory included today's states of Minnesota, Iowa, Wisconsin, and northern Illinois, as well as a considerable region to the west.

Early settlements were thus related to mining rather than agriculture. Many of the early miners were from Kentucky and Missouri and brought with them southern social and political customs. The miner, his pickaxe and a 'pig of lead' have a place on the Wisconsin state flag, a reminder of the early importance of the southwestern corner of the state (see page 4).

As word of fertile soil conditions spread east, an influx of Yankee farmers and Northern Europeans began. This group rapidly became a majority and brought a New York system of local government, featuring the township as the local unit of government. The crest of European immigration to the area came between 1850 and 1900.

There remains today great evidence of the European heritage of the Upper Mississippi in family names, town names, food, festivals and architecture. Various ethnic groups prevail in the many small towns along the Mississippi.

Weather

The weather in the river valley is that of seasonal extremes. The average temperature in January is 16 degrees above 0 (Fahrenheit), but can drop to lows of 40 below or rise to 50 above. During outdoor activities in winter be aware of *chill factor* reports which measure the effect of wind speed and temperature on bare skin. July averages 73 degrees with possible lows of 32 and highs of 102. Generally mild weather is the norm from April through December.

Maritime tropical air from the Gulf of Mexico often wafts its way up the Mississippi River Valley. This accounts for the occasional humidity and fog in the immediate valley area. The unusual *winter fogs* are caused when warm air from the southwestern deserts meets the cold air above the frozen ground. Summer fogs occur when cooler upland air drains down into the valley to collect in warmer bottomlands.

Thunder and lightning storms are quite common in the valley. Severe weather watches are announced regularly on radio and TV. A *watch* indicates that conditions are right for a severe storm to develop. A *warning* indicates there is immediate danger, and shelter should be sought.

For the most part, however, variable conditions prevail. In summer, expect lots of sunshine, cool nights, warm days.

Geology, Geography

The most significant geographical aspect of the Mississippi River Valley (and a primary reason for its great beauty) is that it is a *driftless* or unglaciated peninsula that has been surrounded time and again by glacial advances; yet the deeply dissected valleys, ridges and bluffs were never actually encroached upon by the last iceflows reshaping the rest of North America.

The gently rolling farmland so characteristic of much of Wisconsin and Minnesota is the result of the grinding action and deposits of advancing and receding glaciers. Glacial deposits are referred to as *drift* — a blanket of rich soils and ground rock which is carried and finally deposited by the glacier, its meltwater and the wind. Though not actually covered by glacier, the barren limestone sediments of the valley have been covered by a thick layer of *loess*, a rich, black silt-like layer of soil blown in by the wind from mudflats and river beds as meltwaters receded.

Rather than the granite bedrock found throughout the northern half of Wisconsin, the Mississippi River Valley is comprised mostly of shale, dolomite, and sandstone — sediments laid down by ancient oceans, 300-600 million years ago.

It is the ebb and flow of these oceans which has leveled the tops of the bluffs along the river.

Through the eons, torrents of glacial meltwater have gradually eroded through alternating layers of durable limestone and crumbling sandstone to form the gorge of the Mississippi. The rocky bluffs with sandstone and dolomite layers often clearly visible, soar almost straight up from the valley floor 500 ft. below. These bluffs and occasional rock monuments provide some of the most striking scenery in adjoining states.

River gravel, sand mines and limestone quarries are all encountered as one travels the Great River Road. Rock hounds may be interested to know that the Winona gravel pits are an excellent source of Lake Superior agates. More detailed information is available from lapidary shops located in many of the small towns.

Limestone along the Mississippi River basin is a virtually unlimited resource and is used as a building stone, for agricultural lime, or as crushed rock for concrete construction. Indians used bands of *chert* in the tough dolomite as a substitute for flint. Local limestone quarries provided settlers with stone for buildings which can still be seen in riverside homes, barns, and commercial structures.

The most unusual glacial deposits to be found along the Great River Road are diamonds, found first in Pierce County in the late 1800's. Speculation is that a glacier knocked off the top of a diamond cone somewhere in Canada and carried it into northern Wisconsin where prospecting continues with recent success.

While 70% of the rivers in the state of Wisconsin drain into the Mississippi River via the Chippewa/Flambeau, St. Croix, Black, Rock and Wisconsin rivers, virtually none of the more than 8,800 lakes and ponds in the state are found in the driftless area along the Great River Road. Thus the traveler will find noted in this Guide those towns that offer a public swimming pool.

So savor this portion of your travels. Mother Nature has held it untouched for us — almost since time began.

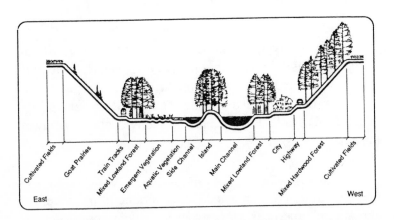

Cross section of the Upper Mississippi River Valley showing typical vegetation and land uses. Sketch is courtesy of the Upper Mississippi River National Wildlife and Fish Refuge and portrays a view to the south with Wisconsin bluffs on the left. Much of the information for this section was from the 1964 Wisconsin Blue Book.

National Scenic Riverway

PIERCE COUNTY

Just east of St. Paul, MN, and the I-494, the green Pilot's Wheel of America's Great River Road directs the traveler to Prescott, WI, on *USH 10*. Prescott's unique lift bridge crosses the St. Croix River just as it joins with the Mississippi.

The St. Croix River has been designated as a *National Scenic Riverway* which means that much of the river is under the protection and management of the National Park Service. It is also home to *Kinnickinnic State Park,* Wisconsin's only state park designed for the enjoyment of boaters. The Mississippi is dotted with inviting sand bars and islands formed by deposits of sediment from the faster moving St. Croix.

Minnesota maintains a tidy beach and park on *Point Douglas* (just before the lift bridge into Prescott) which offers superb views to the north of the St. Croix River.

Just before Point Douglas, on the Minnesota shore, off *STH 10* onto *CTH 21* and to the north about 2 miles, is the unique *Carpenter Saint Croix Valley Nature Center*. Its varied activites include animal rehabilitation, environmental studies and a self-guided trail which in the fall offers excellent viewing of the colors of the river valley. The nature center is open to the public on the first and third Sunday of each month, with activities related to the season.

SPECIAL EVENTS

MAY — *Prescott Arts and Wine Festival*

SEPTEMBER 4th Weekend — *Prescott Daze* - family fun, arts/crafts and sidewalk sales. Soapbox derby and fireman's fights Saturday, parade on Sunday.

CITY OF PRESCOTT
(population 2654)

The city faces the beautiful waterscape formed by the confluence of the St. Croix River on the north side of the bridge and the Mississippi River to the south of the bridge. Big boats, marinas, and crisp nautical garb abound in this little town with a distinct "good time" air about it.

The Prescott waterfront includes an inviting river walkway and a public beach on Lake Street, just north of the *Steamboat Inn,* home port of the *Party Girl* cruise vessel. Several marinas and a public boat launch are just south of Mercord Park (under the lift bridge.) Wisconsin cheeses, fresh bakery, jewelry, antiques, crafts, cafes and fine arts shops are located in the downtown area along the riverfront.

A Brief History of Prescott

The City of Prescott is one of the oldest river towns along the Wisconsin shore. The first permanent dwelling was that of Philander Prescott, an Indian Agent, who built a cabin in 1839. Yankee speculators (who likely were officers at Fort Snelling) hired Prescott to hold their claim to land in the area. They believed that because of the confluence of the two great rivers and nearby Fort Snelling, Prescott would become the major metropolis of the north. Instead, in part because of exorbitant prices the group demanded for their land, St. Paul became the major city.

Early industries included a transport station for logs floated down the St. Croix and Mississippi Rivers, breweries, a brick yard using local clay, a cooperage where barrels were made, flour and grain mills, hotels and sawmills.

Fort Snelling, in St. Paul, MN, was established in 1819 as a frontier outpost and trading center. Through the years, Officers Zachary Taylor (who went on to become President of the United States), William T. Sherman (well known Union General during the civil war), and others served in this northern frontier. Count Ferdinand Zeppelin made his first balloon ascent from fort grounds.

The fort overlooks the Minnesota River and today is a Minnesota State Park just off Interstate 494. Well preserved and maintained much as it was in the early 1800's, it is manned by infantry in period costumes and houses a great number of traditional craftspeople who explain the old methods of making candles and tools, printing and other crafts. The use of cannon, muskets and other weaponry is demonstrated.

TOUR ROUTE: PRESCOTT TO MAIDEN ROCK

PI-1
PRESCOTT BEACH (north end of city, on St. Croix River).
400 ft. of beach front. Lifeguard during authorized hours.
Toilet • water • bathhouse

KINNICKINNIC STATE PARK (north of city, on *USH 10,*
turn north onto *CTH F)*. State park marker is at foot of the first
steep hill, where bridge crosses the Kinnickinnic River. On
west side of road, parking area and foot paths only. An
excellent stop for walkers and birders as foot paths lead to
quiet, sandy spots along the Kinnickinnic and backwaters of
the St. Croix. Most of the park is accessible only to boaters
who can stay overnight either in moored boats or campsites.

The Kinnickinnic is a cold water trout stream, so try
your luck. Wisconsin does require a fishing license and an
inland waters trout stamp for trout fishing in streams and
creeks located all along the Great River Road.

**The Great River Road follows *STH 35* (previously
CTH Q) south through Prescott -- a sharp right on Broad
Street when crossing the lift bridge into Prescott from
Minnesota.**

**12 miles to Diamond Bluff on *STH 35*
25 miles to *USH 63* at Hager City**

PI-2

RIVER WALK (north of Mercord Mill Park, under bridge). A walkway along the Mississippi River bank approximately 20 feet above the river level. Stairs lead to a wooden pier for temporary boat docking. No easy access for trailer-launched boats.   Benches along sidewalk • picnic sites • boat access

PI-3

MERCORD MILL PARK (Foot of Kinnickinnic St., south side of lift bridge). Two acre park. Historical marker with details of Prescott history.   Roofed picnic tables • grills • scenic river view • toilets • water

Mercord Mill Park is directly beside the confluence of the St. Croix and Mississippi rivers. The color line where the blue waters of the St. Croix join the brown waters of the Mississippi is clearly visible. At this point, the Mississippi has already wound its way 520 miles from Lake Itasca near Bemidji, its Minnesota source. The St. Croix has come 150 scenic miles through valleys and canyons carved out by the melt waters of glacial Lake Duluth. For 20 miles to the north, the St. Croix is actually a huge lake, a boater's paradise, formed by the damming effect of sediment settling as the fast moving St. Croix encounters the slower waters of the Mississippi.

PI-4

PRESCOTT JAYCEES BOAT RAMP (south of Mercord Mill Park). Hard-surfaced boat ramp, parking. Honor system coin box for fee charged (currently $4.)

Houseboat rentals at adjacent Mississippi/Croix Harbor marina.

PE-1 — PE-5

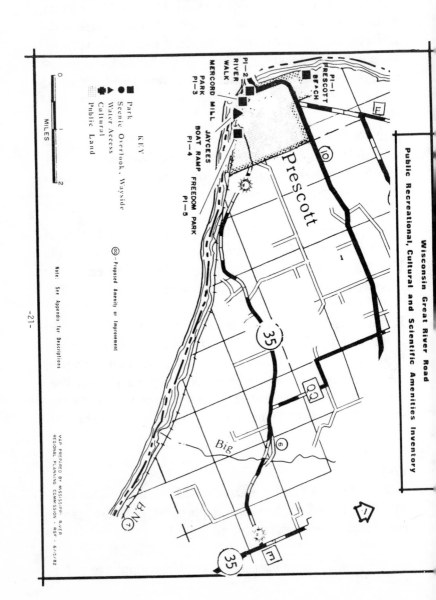

KEY

◼ Park
● Scenic Overlook, Wayside
▲ Water Access
✚ Cultural
▨ Public Land

⊙ — Proposed Amenity or Improvement

Note: See Appendix for Descriptions

Wisconsin Great River Road
Public Recreational, Cultural and Scientific Amenities Inventory

PI-1 PRESCOTT BEACH
PI-2 RIVER WALK
MERCORD MILL PARK PI-3
JAYCEES BOAT RAMP PI-4
FREEDOM PARK PI-5

Prescott

MAP PREPARED BY MISSISSIPPI RIVER
REGIONAL PLANNING COMMISSION - RGF - 6/15/82

PI-5

FREEDOM PARK (Valley View Drive and Monroe St. at the top of the hill on the way south out of town). Named in honor of the eagle released here by staff of the Carpenter Environmental Center. Two-acre park with 14 campsites and scenic view of Mississippi and St. Croix rivers confluence. Fee for camping. Shelter house · picnic grills · playground · electricity

The river views from the Prescott bluffs along STH 35 are stunning at first sight. A pilot once wrote that seen from the air, mountains become ant hills, great lakes become puddles. Only the river takes on added grandeur when seen from on high, as it stretches in serene majesty across the landscape.

The twelve miles from Prescott to Diamond Bluff on *STH 35* is the hilliest portion of the Great River Road in Wisconsin, appearing at times to climb from hill-top to valley bottom and back to the hill-tops. Don't start out low on gas! Just follow the pilot's wheel and enjoy the alternating river and agricultural views.

PI-6

DIAMOND BLUFF LANDING (in community of Diamond Bluff, on *STH 35*, across the railroad tracks). Hard surfaced boat ramp and parking. Broad sand beach near the landing is privately owned -- no swimming please. Instead, visit the beach, deck and docking facilities at *Kask's 1860's Saloon* for real hospitality and comfortable river-watching.

{} **OVERNIGHT RV PARKING** at Kask's Saloon with reduced rates for those traveling with this Guide. Electricity and picnic tables are available for RVers and boaters who may also dock here.

Kask's Saloon is located along the river in an area that was once the local Farmers' Market. Homemade soup, short order food, and the possibility of seeing the elegant paddle-wheelers, the *Delta Queen* or *Mississippi Queen,* pass almost at your feet as you lounge on the deck. A friendly rest stop that is quiet weekdays, busy on weekends.

PI-7

LOCK & DAM #3 visible on Minnesota side. Not accessible from the Wisconsin shore.

Prairie Island Nuclear Plant (on Minnesota side). Warm water discharge from the nuclear plant keeps water from here to Red Wing open for boating year around. Great fishing all year. Boat access at PI-8 on *USH 63* to Red Wing.

PI-8

PUBLIC ACCESS, CAMPING, FOOD (near Hager City, on *USH 63* to Red Wing, MN). There are several boat landings on this short stretch of road which bisects the river bottoms on the way to the bridge over the Main Channel at Red Wing. *Gene's Lounge and Grill* has a new roomy deck area for river watching as well as food and overnight boat dockage. Year around boat access from the SHANTY CAMPGROUND. THE ISLAND CAMPGROUND is located just before the bridge to Red Wing. Both campgrounds offer electricity, river's edge camping, and dump station.

THE AMERICAN MUSEUM OF WILDLIFE ART has relocated from Frontenac, to Red Wing, MN, and is now located northwest of town at the corner of *USH 61* and Tyler Road. Exhibits of original wildlife paintings by living and deceased wildlife artists. Look for **This Quiet Dust,** an historical novel about early Frontenac, in the museum shop.

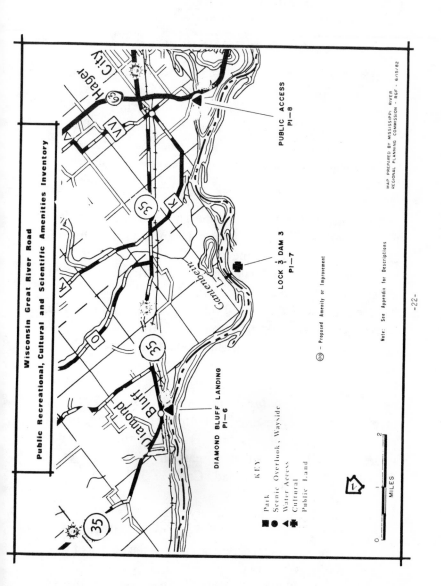

Wisconsin Great River Road
Public Recreational, Cultural and Scientific Amenities Inventory

Hager City

PUBLIC ACCESS
PI—8

LOCK & DAM 3
PI—7

DIAMOND BLUFF LANDING
PI—6

Crapacient

Diamond Bluff

KEY

■ Park
● Scenic Overlook, Wayside
▲ Water Access
✣ Cultural
✣ Public Land

◎ — Proposed Amenity or Improvement

Note: See Appendix for Descriptions

MAP PREPARED BY MISSISSIPPI RIVER
REGIONAL PLANNING COMMISSION - RGF - 6/15/82

MILES

0   2

-22-

TOUR ROUTE: HAGER CITY, WI, TO RED WING AND
FRONTENAC, MN ON *USH 63*

RED WING, MINNESOTA

This Minnesota city features an expanding turn-of-the-century Main Street restoration capped by the elegant *St. James Hotel*. Built in 1875, it was purchased in 1977 by the Red Wing Shoe Company. Each of the rooms, half of which have river views, is individually furnished with antiques and collectibles. Several unique boutiques and restaurants are located within.

Outside the St. James, the authentic San Francisco trolley car *The Spirit of Red Wing* begins a narrated historical sightseeing tour of the city. The *City of Red Wing* excursion paddlewheeler leaves Levee Park behind the St. James about 1 p.m. each day between Memorial Day and mid-October. The well-developed walking tour is an education in domestic architecture dating from the 1850's to the 1870's. A descriptive brochure is available at the front desk of the St. James.

The *T.B. Sheldon Auditorium Theatre,* of 1904 vintage, has been fully restored and offers a broad range of live performances, exhibitions, and classical cinema. This intimate, "Jewel Box" of a theatre seats only 470, however, so reservations are recommended. Call 612-388-2806.

The old *Red Wing Pottery factory* has been closed since 1967 but is now open as a shopping mall with many interesting boutiques. There is golfing in the center of town at the Red Wing Country Club and several riverside parks are located just off *USH 61*. *Colville Park* has a swimming pool.

A Brief History of Red Wing

The bright red wings which have decorated so many locally produced products were also the trade mark of the Sioux Chief, *Red Wing,* who supposedly wore the red-dyed wings of a swan as his headdress. It may have been his daughter, We-no-nah (namesake of the city of Winona) who leaped to her death at Maiden Rock *though poor We-no-nah has been linked to every chief and lofty bluff face along the river!*

The city of Red Wing is located at the foot of Barn Bluff which once existed as an island sculpted by the Glacial River Warren. It was settled in the 1840's by Scandinavian immigrants and by 1873 had become the primary wheat market in the world. Alexander P. Anderson, the inventor of *puffed wheat* and *puffed rice* made his home here. The Goodhue County Historical Museum is located on College Hill.

FRONTENAC, MINNESOTA

About 10 miles south of Red Wing on *USH 61,* are found *Old Frontenac, Frontenac,* and *Frontenac State Park.* The park is located on the approximate site of *Fort Beauharnois,* the last fort established by the French along the Upper Mississippi. Its chapel, built in 1727, is considered to be the site of the first Christian chapel in Minnesota.

New Frontenac sprang up around the railroad depot after the railroad was granted an easement about two miles inland of the old town. Today it is a small settlement along the east side of *USH 61.* An outlet store, a small cafe, and a few supplies are available.

Old Frontenac was established in 1839 as a trading post known as Waconia. It was renamed Frontenac in 1859 in honor of *Count Frontenac,* the Governor of New France (the North American territories) from 1671-1698.

As one of the few river towns which did not sacrifice its waterfront to the railroads, Old Frontenac soon became a resort town known nationally as the ''Newport of the Northwest.'' Wealthy visitors from New Orleans, St. Louis, and St. Paul came to stay at the Lakeside Hotel. The quiet village still resembles a tiny Cape Cod residential resort town, right to the pristine white Gatsby-like estates overlooking Lake Pepin. There are no commercial establishments.

Those who have admired the chateaux in France (or the castles on the Rhine) will be transported by the sudden, massive appearance of *Villa Maria,* once a highly regarded convent school for girls established in 1891. The adjacent wooden academy burned in 1969, but the Villa remains open as a retreat and workshop center. It is still operated by the Ursuline Sisters, who arrived in 'New France' in 1727. The oldest building on the Mississippi is an Ursuline convent built in 1744 and located in New Orleans.

The privately operated *Mount Frontenac* offers downhill skiing and an 18-hole golf course. Cross-country skiers can find groomed trails at Frontenac State Park. The park offers excellent birding, snowmobiling, hiking, and camping.

LAKE CITY, MN, is located six miles south of Frontenac on the Great River Road, *USH 61*. See page 33.

Return to Hager City, WI, where the Great River Road
joins *STH 35*.

PI-9
BOW & ARROW HISTORICAL SITE (pullover along Great
River Road). Historical Marker describes speculation as to
meaning of the bow and arrow *boulder effigy* clearly visible
on bluff-side. Current theory is that it represents a flying bird
rather than a bow and arrow. Attributed to completely un-
known Indian culture.

PI-10
BAY CITY (population 453) VILLAGE PARK (head of Lake
Pepin in village). Hard-surfaced boat launch. Quiet, well
maintained village *camping* area directly on the large bay.
Small fee. Parking • picnicking • toilets • water • camping •
RV dump station

BAY CITY SILICA MINE. Established in 1919, the mine
operates right alongside the Great River Road just south of
Bay City. Silica is a very hard sand that is actually mined from
inside the bluff, washed, and sold mainly for sandblasting.
The fairly simple operation is easily seen with a very short,
level walk from the parking area. On a hot day, the 54 degree
air gushing from the mine is a real treat.

PI-11
LAKE PEPIN WAYSIDE PARK (*STH 35* approximately 1-
1/2 miles west of Maiden Rock). Scenic views of Lake Pepin
portion of river. The craggy, tree-topped bluffs we see today
look almost identical to what the early French explorers saw
200 years ago. Trail access to Lake Pepin. Picnic tables •
grills • parking • toilets • water

Note the large chunks of fossil-embedded local lime-stone at each wayside. Early settlers quarried this abundant rock for building and to sell to the government for dam construction along the river as it was developed for commercial shipping. Many of the early roads were paved by hauling the limestone onto the roadbed where it was smashed into gravel with hand-wielded sledge hammers.

PI-12
LAKE PEPIN OVERLOOK and Historical Marker (just south of PI-11). Scenic river views. Historical marker describes Lake Pepin portion of the Mississippi River.

PI-13
RUSH RIVER FISHERMAN PARKING (large paved area east of *STH 35.*) Walk-in access to Rush River. Approximately 1/2 mile via Rush River to Lake Pepin. Scenic drive on *CTH A.*

PI-14
MAIDEN ROCK CAMPGROUND AND PICNIC AREA (in village of Maiden Rock, on Mississippi River). Access to Lake Pepin via non-surfaced boat launch is suitable only for small boats as water is very shallow. *Camping* area with 4 electric sites. Pay small fee in deposit box at limestone Senior Citizen building beside the unguarded railroad tracks. Picnic tables • grills

The limestone building facing the park in Maiden Rock is one of the oldest in the village. The park itself was the former dock area. A packet boat (which carried freight, passengers, animals, entertainers - just about anything) once brought supplies from Frontenac, MN. Many of the early settlers, like those from neighboring Stockholm, came from Sweden.

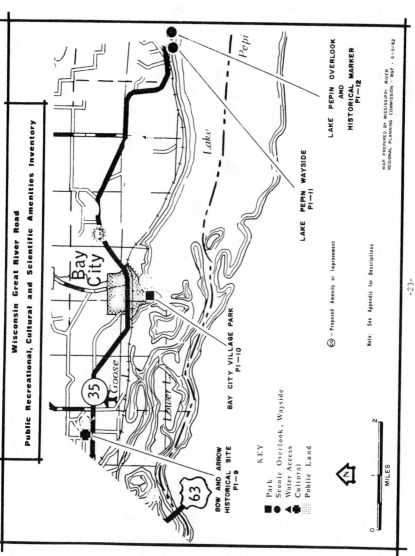

Wisconsin Great River Road
Public Recreational, Cultural and Scientific Amenities Inventory

Lake Pepi

Lake

Lake Pepin Overlook and Historical Marker PI-12

Lake Pepin Wayside PI-11

Bay City

Bay City Village Park PI-10

Goose L.

Lower L.

35

63

Bow and Arrow Historical Site PI-9

KEY

■ Park
● Scenic Overlook, Wayside
▲ Water Access
✽ Cultural
▦ Public Land

(PI) — Proposed Amenity or Improvement

Note: See Appendix for Descriptions

MAP PREPARED BY MISSISSIPPI RIVER REGIONAL PLANNING COMMISSION - RGF - 6/15/82

N

0   1   2
MILES

A 400-DOLL COLLECTION is on display in the IGA store. Antiques are for sale at the historic Mercantile Building on the south end of the village.

Historic Maiden Rock School
Built with Locally Quarried Limestone
Sketch by Nelson Brown

PI-15
FISHERMAN PARKING AREA (on *STH 35* at Pierce-Pepin County line, on Pine Creek). Short walk across railroad tracks to the Mississippi River.

PE-1
MAIDEN ROCK OVERLOOK WAYSIDE (Two miles south of Pepin County Line). Scenic view of Lake Pepin. See *Lake City* across Lake Pepin, the bluff of Maiden Rock directly down river on the Wisconsin side and *Point-No-Point* which seems to extend into the river to the south. As you exit the wayside, glance up at the wind-sculpted sandstone cliffs directly overhead. More park than wayside. Grills· picnic tables · water · toilets

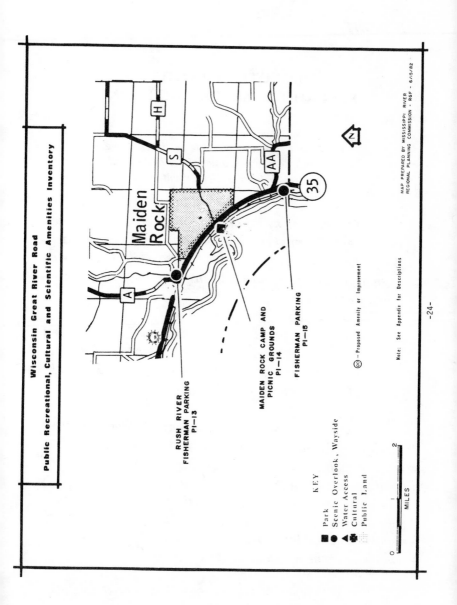

Wisconsin Great River Road

Public Recreational, Cultural and Scientific Amenities Inventory

Maiden Rock

RUSH RIVER
FISHERMAN PARKING
PI—13

MAIDEN ROCK CAMP AND
PICNIC GROUNDS
PI—14

FISHERMAN PARKING
PI—15

KEY

■ Park
● Scenic Overlook, Wayside
▲ Water Access
✿ Cultural
▦ Public Land

⊚ — Proposed Amenity or Improvement

Note: See Appendix for Descriptions

MAP PREPARED BY MISSISSIPPI RIVER
REGIONAL PLANNING COMMISSION - RGF - 6/15/82

MILES
0   1   2

-24-

INSIGHT

DOROTHY GANNETT
STOCKHOLM ARTISTS' GUILD, INC.

The Lake Pepin area ought to be visited in the summer by every poet and painter in the land.
- William Cullen Bryant

On considering Bryant's observation, one is tempted to comment, "He ought to have been here the rest of the year." Winter here, with its brilliant blue skies and sparkling fields of snow, can be even more awe-inspiring than the leisurely passing of summer!

Painters, poets, musicians, fine artists, and craftspeople have been living year around in the Lake Pepin area for many years, drawing inspiration from the lake, the hills and woods, the rivers and coulees.

An artist's history of the Maiden Rock/Stockholm area begins in the late 60's and early 70's. At that time, a considerable number of aspiring young artists and craftspeople, many of them graduates of the Minneapolis College of Art and Design, found their way into the region around Lake Pepin. They made their homes in drafty, uninsulated old farmhouses in and around the tiny villages and back in the wooded hills and coulees.

Living conditions were often primitive, without electricity, indoor plumbing or central heating. Those who were hardy and dedicated worked at their arts and crafts, and started families. Living conditions improved little by little as they eked out a meager income from arts and crafts shows during the spring and summer.

It was a small group of these artists who banded together in 1974 to begin the now popular Stockholm Art Fair. Today, the Stockholm Artists' Guild, Inc., is putting its considerable determination behind the renovation of the Maiden Rock School into a Community Arts Center and Gallery. The Arts Center will provide local artists with greater exposure for their work, as well as a home base for fostering greater interest in all the arts: literary, performing, and visual.

Maybe it's sentimental, but, for those of us who call ourselves artists, there is a magic in the expansive views from high atop a hill or river bluff and in the winding, tree-shaded country roads that require three land miles to travel one mile's distance. As times get better (for artists seem always to start out poor) the plumbing will come.

Ice Fishing Shanties, painting by Marion Biehn

"Little House" Country

PEPIN COUNTY

Only a short scenic portion of Pepin County borders the Mississippi River. *STH 35,* Wisconsin's Great River Road, hugs the bluffs along the edge of Lake Pepin and every point offers a new panorama of abundant water, tree covered rocky bluffs, and a broad expanse of sky. The 20 miles along Lake Pepin and through the villages of Stockholm and Pepin is considered to be one of the most scenic drives in the midwest.

The shores of Lake Pepin were first explored and exploited by the French during the 1600's. Furs and European goods were traded between white man and Indian. *Fort St. Antoine* was built just south of the current village of Stockholm by Nicholas Perrot as the base from which the French conducted business and administered the territory. In 1689, Perrot formally claimed the entire Northwest for Louis the 14th, King of France.

The first log home in the county was built in 1856. In 1867, Laura Ingalls Wilder was born in a log cabin 7 miles northwest of the village of Pepin. Her first book, written when she was sixty-five, was *Little House in the Big Woods*. It was the first in a series of eight *Little House* books and describes her experiences in the Pepin area.

SPECIAL EVENTS

Last weekend in JAN	Lake City, *Winterfest*, winter golf classic, parade of cutters and sleighs. Gourmet Food & Beverage Fest, Fireworks 'on ice.' Torchlight snowmobile parade, craft fair.
3rd Saturday in JULY	*Stockholm Art Fair*, Stockholm Park. Juried arts/crafts sale.
Last full weekend in JUNE	Lake City, *Waterski Days*, Waterski shows, professional entertainment, arts/crafts fair, carnival, antique cars, Venetian boat parade.

LAKE PEPIN

One of the most scenic pools on the river, Lake Pepin formed naturally for twenty miles upstream from where the Chippewa River meets the Mississippi. As the sediment from the swifter moving Chippewa settled, it formed a sandy delta --a natural dam--in the path of the sluggish Mississippi.

Today Lake Pepin is a boater's paradise and wildlife haven. Seen mostly from the bluff tops, the river-lake is speckled with white sails, the spray from motorboats, and the whitecaps of waves that can spring up almost without warning. On more than one occasion, early steamboats floundered in sudden storms, and passengers found themselves spilled into great swells and waves from which some never escaped.

The most disasterous sinking on Lake Pepin was that of the excursion boat *Sea Wing* which overturned during a storm in July 1890. Despite courageous rescue attempts illuminated only by lightening strikes, half of the two hundred passengers lost their lives.

TOUR ROUTE: STOCKHOLM TO PEPIN, WI, ON STH 35

Point-No-Point, extending into Lake Pepin from the Minnesota shore, was named by river boat pilots who used this "point" of land as a navigational landmark. In fact, it is not a point at all. The "point" effect is an optical illusion caused by a continuing curve of land. The effect is visible if you care to keep an eye on Point-No-Point as you drive south.

Mark Twain describes this point in **Old Times on the Mississippi.** *"I would fasten my eyes upon a sharp, wooded point that projected far into the river some miles ahead of me, . . .and just as we would draw up toward it, the exasperating thing would begin to melt away and fold back into the bank."*

LAKE CITY, MN, is a beautiful city with extensive riverside parks and the largest small-boat harbor on the Mississippi. Camping, motels, and riverside dining are all available to the traveler.

The sport of water-skiing was invented here in 1922 when an avid downhill skier formed two ski-like boards and arranged to be pulled by a motorboat. The original boards may still be seen at the Chamber of Commerce office across the street from the marina. The excursion paddlewheeler, *Spirit of Lake City,* follows the historic packet route between Lake City and Stockholm, with dinner cruises and a Sunday brunch available. Wild Wings Gallery, located 1/2 mile south of the city on *USH 61,* offers wildlife art, prints, books, and gifts for sale. Bald eagles winter along the shores of Lake Pepin and from January to March are easily spotted from numerous waysides south of Lake City.

HOK-SI-LA CITY PARK (located just north of Lake City on *USH 61)* is a former Boy Scout Camp that offers camping, hiking, picnicking, and swimming with over two miles of beach and shoreline. Vehicles are limited to the parking area.

Broad river-lakes, or 'pools' form up-river of each lock or natural dam formed by sedimentation.

PE-2
MAIDEN ROCK HISTORIC SITE (1/2 mile north of Stockholm village limits). Historical Marker describes the Maiden Rock Indian Legend. Rock is located above wayside, directly across the highway. (No amenities at PE-3)

PE-4
STOCKHOLM VILLAGE PARK (in Village of Stockholm). 2 acres. Hard surfaced boat ramp. Undesignated swimming area. Primitive *camping* with $5 fee. 10 sites with electricity. The excursion boat, *Spirit of Lake City*, docks at the park. Ball diamond · shelter house · picnicking · water · toilets

Notice the high-water mark on trees in the park. Water levels have varied by as much as 14 feet in recent years. Trees are fenced to protect from "girdling" by beaver. Beaver will chew the bark away around even very large trees which will kill the tree.

WISCONSIN'S LITTLE SWEDEN

Stockholm, with its population of 104, is proof that bigger is not necessarily better. Here is a must-stop destination along the Great River Road.

For campers, there is a well-developed *Village Campground,* beach, boat launch and park across the railroad tracks. The Hotel at the north edge of town was built of native limestone in 1864 and has four rooms that have been carefully restored to retain the spirit of days gone by. A second limestone building on the south end of town was built in 1878 and houses the *Stockholm Cafe* which specializes in locally produced food and beverages.

So make yourself at home. Each well-kept, well preserved little building has a special surprise for the leisurely traveler. This is an artist's community, and the one-block business district in Wisconsin's sixth smallest village may be among the most interesting to be found anywhere.

Within this block, one will find a *fine arts and crafts gallery* run by a man who came here after living in Africa. Besides displaying the exceptional work of several local artists, he also sells hand-made baskets from Botswana, Africa. Next door, a French-Moroccan woman who studied art and design in Paris runs the only known jewelry store in the world which specializes in handcrafted jewelry designed around native Mississippi freshwater pearls. Travelers are welcome to visit the *Mississippi Pearl Jewelry Company* to see this native river jewelry.

Across the street, in a huge turn of the century shop, are quilts, folk arts, and furnishings, all created by *Amish* craftspeople. Nearby is the *Stockholm Institute* and heritage museum. This non-profit organization maintains a museum and archives preserving the history of Stockholm and a record of the Swedish heritage of the area.

Two unique *market gardens* near the village supply much of the seasonal produce used in the Cafe. One of these is run by a man who studied agriculure in mainland China; the other by a couple recently involved in archaeological studies in Alaska. The old-fashioned country store on the north end of town provides everything from hand-dipped ice cream cones and groceries to guns and gasoline.

The annual **Stockholm Art Fair** attracts more than 110 juried exhibitors and 5000 visitors to town during the third weekend in July.

PE-5
WAYSIDE (Junction of *STH 35* & *CTH JJ*, south of town). Very nice park, on left just after turning onto *CTH JJ*. Picnic grills · tables · water · toilets

PE-6
FORT ST. ANTOINE SITE, SCENIC OVERLOOK (1 mile southeast of Stockholm). Historical Marker commemorating site of Fort built in 1686 by Nicholas Perrot. No direct water access.

THE FRENCH ERA
1634 - 1763

For nearly 125 years, the French laid claim to the Upper Mississippi. It was the French explorers, fur traders, missionary priests, and government agents who set the names and sites of many of the oldest settlements.

In 1634 Jean Nicolet, under the direction of the great explorer, La Salle, canoed the Fox River out of Green Bay and into the interior of present-day Wisconsin. Intent on finding a northwest passage to the Pacific, he was the first European to learn from the native Indians of a great river to the west which they called *Miche Sepi.*

In 1671 Nicholas Perrot gathered the chiefs of area Indian tribes near Sault St. Marie to formally announce that they were under the protection of France and Count Frontenac, Governor of New France. A short time later, Louis Joliet and Father James Marquette were the first to enter the Mississippi via the *Ouisconsin* (Wisconsin) River in June 1673. They were eager to report that it was possible to canoe the entire distance from Green Bay to the Mississippi with only one short land portage (near Portage, WI).

Many of the explorers who followed have left their names along the Mississippi: Daniel Greysolon Du Lhut (Duluth) and Rev. Louis Hennepin were the first to thoroughly explore the northern-most reaches of the Mississippi and St. Croix rivers during the late 1670's. Nicholas Perrot and his command of twenty men built Fort St. Antoine in 1686 to help enforce France's claim to all lands west of the Mississippi.

The French, however, were explorers, missionaries and traders, not farmers or soldiers. As late as 1760, when France ceded this portion of New France to England after the French and Indian War, there were still no permanent settlements along the Mississippi River. French traders had permanent cabins in the vicinity of many of today's river towns (e.g. Trempealeau, DeSoto, Genoa, Prairie du Chien), but no permanent residents.

The English explorer, Jonathan Carver, records in 1766 that *Les Prairies des Chiens* (the Dog Plains) was a thriving Indian village of 300 permanent families. The current sites of Wabasha, La Crosse and Nelson were busy trading centers.

In 1783, four white persons set up permanent residence at Prairie du Chien, which meant that when England yielded possession of the Mississippi to America in 1796, there were only two settlements in the entire territory—Green Bay and Prairie du Chien.

PE-7
DEER ISLAND BOAT RAMP (upstream end of Deer Island, approximately three miles west of village of Pepin). Hard-surfaced boat ramp with parking.

PE-8
LAKEPORT OVERLOOK (west side of village of Pepin). Undeveloped.

PE-9

LAURA INGALLS WILDER PARK (Main Street, village of Pepin). Not located on the waterfront. State Historical Marker commemorates birthplace of children's book author, Laura Ingalls Wilder. Birth site is located seven miles north of village at PE-12. Pleasant spot to stop, with convenient parking. Picnic tables • grills • shelter • playground • water • toilets

PEPIN RAILROAD DEPOT MUSEUM is also located in the park under the enthusiastic direction of honorary Depot Agent, William Swanson. Mr. Swanson is more than happy to share with visitors his considerable knowledge of local and railroad history. No fee.

PE-10

MUNICIPAL BEACH (east side of village, adjacent to Marina). Beach with lifeguard. Toilets, showers in adjacent marina service building.

PE-11

PEPIN MARINA. Hard surfaced boat ramp with fee charged to non-residents of the village. Service building with snacks, showers, toilet and parking. Piers • boat services • village courtesy dock

Harborview Cafe on First Street in the village of Pepin, overlooks the marina. Many motels, antique shops and campgrounds are also available nearby.

PEPIN HISTORICAL MUSEUM is maintained by the Laura Ingalls Wilder Society on the east end of town along *STH 35*. Displays of historical artifacts, tools, and Wilder memorabilia.

PE-12
LAURA INGALLS WILDER BIRTH SITE (7 miles from village on *STH 183*). A recently built log cabin representing the type of cabin in which Wilder was born is on this site. Water • toilets • picnic tables

PE-13
FISHERMAN PARKING AREA (between Chippewa River and Village of Nelson on *STH 35*). Adjacent to Swinger Slough. Informal parking.

Between Pepin and Nelson (7 miles), the Great River Road traverses the extensive Nelson Bottoms, including the *Tiffany Wildlife Area* and the Chippewa River at the Pepin/Buffalo County line. Until the 1930's, the railroad provided the only land transportation through this wilderness area.

The opposite of a 'pool' are the many islands and sloughs often found below the dams.

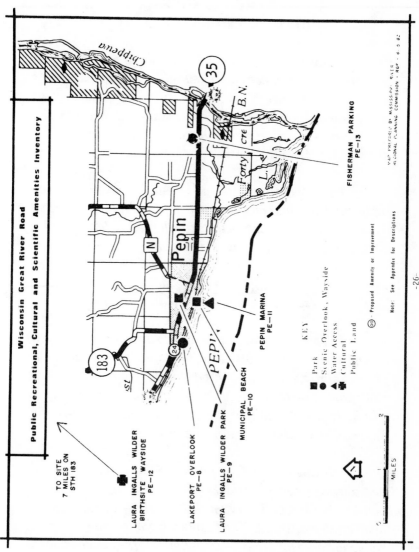

Wisconsin Great River Road

Public Recreational, Cultural and Scientific Amenities Inventory

TO SITE
7 MILES ON
STH 183

LAURA INGALLS WILDER
BIRTHSITE WAYSIDE
PE-12

LAKEPORT OVERLOOK
PE-8

LAURA INGALLS WILDER PARK
PE-9

MUNICIPAL BEACH
PE-10

PEPIN MARINA
PE-11

FISHERMAN PARKING
PE-13

KEY

Park
Scenic Overlook, Wayside
Water Access
Cultural
Public Land

Note: See Appendix for Descriptions

(00) - Proposed Amenity or Improvement

MAP PREPARED BY MISSISSIPPI RIVER
REGIONAL PLANNING COMMISSION - RGF - 6 5 82

MILES

Pepin

Chippewa

-26-

INSIGHT

FRED LESHER
BIRDER AND NATURALIST

My own philosophical approach to our environment is that Americans can not continue to think like pioneers. It's been 100 years since Wisconsin was truly a frontier, yet we continue to act as if our resources are unlimited: every last bit of wilderness must be tamed, cultivated, developed, marketed, and sold for a profit.

This is what I call a frontier mentality, an emphasis on Individualism that is no longer appropriate. It is unlikely that our economy can maintain the growth rate we have become accustomed to and the economic slow down we are experiencing now is likely just a preview. Personal restraint, the kind which the Japanese and others have had to cultivate for hundreds of years because of their population, is new to us.

It's natural to think that we can do whatever we have brains, technology, money to do; but we cannot continue to exhaust our resources. I don't advocate 'going back' — we can't go back — but we do have to restrain the way we behave. The more intellectually informed we are about nature, the better we may adjust our expectations.

Birding is very different from going to a country club and playing golf. One thinks of golf as being an outdoors activity, but it's still very much INSIDE — cultured, well-mannered, cultivated. The best birding often takes place in rather uncared for areas — areas that others often consider to be 'wasteland' that should be 'better utilized.'

F.L.

Gateway to the Northern Forests

BUFFALO COUNTY

As early as 1680, the Jesuit explorer Father Louis Hennepin was referring to the Chippewa River by its Indian name, the *Buffalo River*. He noted then that it was "full of turtles." Over 100 years later an account by Thomas G. Anderson, who spent 50 years in the area as fur trader and Indian Agent, again refers to the Buffalo River.

Buffalo County was part of the winter grazing area for the huge herds of buffalo which scoured the northern plains. Anderson refers to seeing tens of thousands of buffalo within the Mississippi River valley. At times, he wrote, the earth seemed to quiver and shake, not with pounding hooves, but from the "angry bellowing of 10,000 bulls." Another time, he mentions the northern bay of Lake Pepin as being "black with swimming buffalo."

The Indians in the early 1800's were still desperately dependent upon buffalo for food and shelter. Anderson notes that the unusually warm winter of 1807 meant that few buffalo moved as far south as Lake Pepin and the natives experienced wholesale starvation. "This spring over 40 Indian bodies were found in the Buffalo (Chippewa) River and it was speculated that they died of starvation trying to find turtles hibernating in the mud."

INSIGHT

ORMA REMEMBERS NELSON

What I remember about my childhood in Nelson are the bluffs. That was before the lock & dam system flooded the bottoms around Nelson — the town was not on the water at all.

The bluffs always provided the young people with something to do. We'd hike to the tops, collect wild-flowers, picnic, cook corn over campfires. The farmers never seemed to mind that we were on their land or picked their walnuts.

The bluffs were full of caves, and I remember wiggling through some of them on my stomach, they were that small. I know people talked of rattlesnakes, but I never saw one. I guess we could have been bitten, or fallen off a ledge while climbing the bluffs, but no one was ever hurt.

There was a rumor of treasure buried by soldiers in the bluffs. Often, people just went up and dug around in their spare time hoping to find it. I never heard that any treasure was ever found.

I remember Armistice Day, November 11, in 1940. We lost several duck hunters that day. I was driving to Iron Creek where I taught school. I always stopped on the way to pick up some of my school children. They were so excited about the search parties going out into the bottoms looking for duck hunters.

The day had started out warm and beautiful. Duck hunters and fishermen had gone out only with light jackets and shirts. Then the wind picked up, the temperature fell below zero. The waves capsized many of the boats. Many hunters were able to make it to islands, but were not rescued until morning. Some died of exposure. No one was dressed for the sub-zero conditions.

My father was a railroad telegrapher and station agent for the Burlington Railroad. His first job was in Stoddard, WI. As the company began closing many of the stations in the smaller towns, he was sent to Trevino, a lever station situated in the bottoms between the towns of Nelson and Pepin. There was no road for motor cars between Pepin and Nelson at that time. The only way to get to his station was on a motor car on the tracks.

At Trevino, the incoming trains had to be switched from double track to single track (in order to cross the bridge) and then back onto double tracks. The railroad bridge had been built when there was just a single track along the river.

The passenger train that ran along the river from Minneapolis/St. Paul was made up of a few passenger cars, baggage car, coal car and an engine we called the 'Puddle Jumper.' Because my father was a railroad man we got free passes to ride on it. That's how we got to the big cities to go shopping.

People did a lot of commercial clamming then in Lake Pepin and along the river. Kettles dotted the shorelines where *the clams were boiled to open the shells. Empty shells were heaped along the shore.*

My mother told about 'toe clamming' in Stoddard. She would walk along the shore in the shallow water feeling for clams with her toes. She often showed me the good pearl she had mounted on a ring. Buyers would visit the clammers to buy their harvest of pearls, slugs and 'chicken feed' (tiny pearl-like material).

That's pretty much what I remember about Nelson. I guess my thoughts always go back to the bluffs.

NELSON, WISCONSIN

The village of Nelson provides all amenities: motels, cafes, restaurants, and gas. *The Nelson Cheese Factory* is conveniently located along *STH 35*. Visitors are invited to tour the factory and enjoy free samples of fresh Wisconsin cheese.

Good Old Nelson Days are held in early August with a parade, barbeque dinners, side-walk sales and ball-games.

Castleberg Park is located on the south end of town, along *STH 35* (not on the river). Shelter house • picnicking • toilets • grills • playground

The prairie on the south end of town was once a meeting place for Indians who engaged in games and trading. Today it is a good source of arrowheads.

TOUR ROUTE: NELSON, WI, TO WABASHA, MN

BU-1, BU-2, BU-3
PONTOON SLOUGH LANDING & WAYSIDE; INDIAN SLOUGH
LANDING & WAYSIDE; BEEF SLOUGH LANDING & WAYSIDE.
(All located on *STH 25* southwest of Nelson.) Gravel surface
boat ramps.

STH 25 to Wabasha, MN stretches across the magnificent Nelson Bottoms, almost 40 square miles of virgin Mississippi River bottomland — sloughs, islands, dense forest, prairie and marshland. Abundant bird and animal life.

WABASHA, MINNESOTA

Wabasha, Minnesota's oldest city, provides the traveler with an interesting stopover. The town's brick commercial district has changed little since the turn of the century. The *Anderson House*, Minnesota's oldest operating hotel, offers fine dining in Grandma's parlor and optional feline bedwarmers in the room. *Great River houseboat rentals* are available at the large marina south of town.

The village is named after the *Wapasha* family of Dakota (Sioux) Indian Chiefs. At the time of the Black Hawk Wars, this was the site of an Indian settlement known as Wapasha's Village.

KRUGER RECREATION AREA (1/2 mile south, off County Road 81 out of Wabasha, MN). Set deep within the Richard J. Dorer Memorial Hardwood State Forest, this area provides campsites, fishing, miles of hiking trails and access to the

Zumbro River, a Minnesota State Canoe Route. Canoe rentals and shuttle services are available.

ARROWHEAD BLUFF EXHIBIT, located 1/2 mile west of *STH 61* at the top of the bluff overlooking the river valley at Wabasha. Exhibit includes wildlife, a complete collection of Winchester guns, artifacts and gifts. Beautiful vistas near the blufftop.

Return to Wisconsin *STH 35*

The drive south on Wisconsin STH 35 from Nelson to Fountain City is another "most scenic" portion of the Great River Road. One hardly knows whether to marvel most at the rocky bluffs looming overhead or the verdant bottomland shading the wide river valley far below. It is important to remember that this is a State Highway, and we must also watch the road! Best to stop at one of the numerous waysides to soak up the scenery!

BU-4
BEEF SLOUGH WAYSIDE (1 mile north of Alma in city limits). State Historical Society marker telling significance of Beef Slough. Overlook of river. Nice, quiet picnic spot with good shore fishing prospects. Two picnic tables • grills

BU-5
WAYSIDE. Scenic Overlook. Turn around is a bit tight for any large vehicle. Grills • no tables • no water

BU-6
BEEF RIVER LANDING (within city limits on Buffalo Slough. Gravel boat ramp. Directly across from Rieck's Lake Park.

BU-7
RIECK'S LAKE PARK (east side of *STH 35* on Buffalo Slough just north of Alma city limits). Large general purpose park situated on edge of backwater lake. 20+ campsites with electricity. Self-registration. Camp right on the water and fish under bridge at south end of campground.   Observe herons and egrets stalking next meal in backwater. Playground • toilets • 14 picnic sites • shelter house • water

The road between Nelson and Alma seems to hopscotch along over numerous marshes, woodlands and prairie areas. At times, the roadway is etched into the bluffside, at times the bluffs sweep away from the Great River Road in a grand semi-circle. Always, the railroad runs alongside.

A towboat pushes its raft of barges past the city of Alma, WI.

BU-1 — BU-6

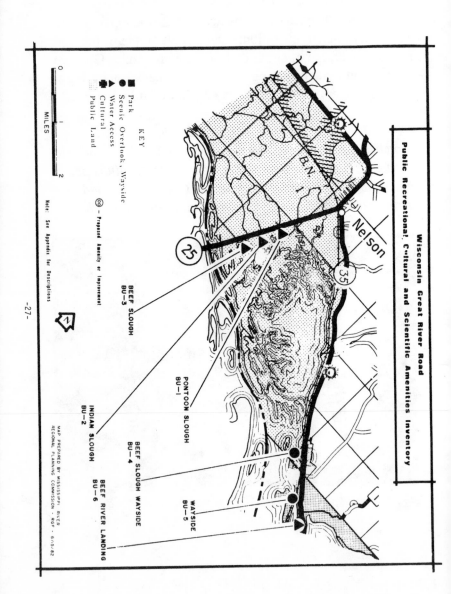

CITY OF ALMA

Like a lazy cat against a sunlit wall, the historic city of Alma stretches for seven miles along the river below towering Twelve Mile Bluff. The many turn-of-the-century frame and brick houses along its two streets have led to much of the town being placed on the National Register of Historic Places. Two restored Bed & Breakfast inns (the *Gallery House* and the *Laue House)* have also been placed on the National Register.

The main bluff behind the town was named by river pilots who could see it from 12 miles north at the mouth of the Chippewa River. Alma may have been named after a river town in Russia. Alma was chosen, according to one story, for its simple spelling and pronunciation.

Many interesting antique and craft shops are located along its extended Main Street. The watercolor originals of resident artist, John Runions, are displayed at the *Riverside Gallery and Spice Shop* at 215 N. Main. Runions' paintings of the *Delta Queen* are familiar to many river buffs. Original works by a variety of local artists are on display at the nearby *Grace Gallery and Ice Cream Shop.* From May to September, the Ice Cream Shop's outdoor garden, set against a stone terrace, makes a delightfully cool rest stop.

A self-guided walking tour of historic Alma is available at the Spice Shop or the Buffalo County Historical Society on 2nd Street between Hill and Oak Steets. Walkers will soon find that most of the 'streets' connecting Main and Second are not streets at all, but stairways up the bluffside! A City Directory and park have been developed mid-town, at the foot of Pine and Main, just above the new city courtesy docks.

Buena Vista Park, located above town on *CTH E,* offers a spectacular overview of the Lock & Dam operation and the islands and sloughs north of the dam. Note the dike dissecting the river, leading all river water to the dam. No one is quite sure why the main slough in the area is called the Wiggle Waggle.

One of the pleasures of a visit to Alma is staying at the *Laue House* at 1111 South Main. This refreshing experience in river town hospitality begins with a note in the hallway inviting one and all to find a room with a key in the door and make oneself at home. Proprietors Gerald and Jan Schreiber are attractions in themselves. Both (yes, both!) have been commercial fishermen and have many good stories if you can take some time to chat. The Schreiber's also operate the Pier 4 diner, a good stop for fresh river catfish. Dinners are served at The Burlington Hotel at the north end of the historic district, though it may not be advertised.

The Mississippi is the only inland waterway serving both as a national transportation corridor and as a national wildlife refuge.

A Bit of Alma History

This area was first settled by Swiss immigrants who moved north from the Galena-Dubuque area with the intention of cutting cordwood to sell passing steamboats for fuel. In 1855, many of the settlers were coming directly from Switzerland and Germany. Most of the early industries dealt with river life--hotels, breweries, logging, and wheat shipping.

At the end of the century, the railroad was built along Alma's riverfront, literally separating the town from its river traffic. Frederick Laue and his saw mill operation were at the heart of the logging boom days. Dr. Arnold Gesell, who founded the Gesell Institute of Child Development in New Haven, CT, is Alma's most famous native son.

BU-8

ALMA MARINA & BEACH (on Buffalo Slough, just north of city) 40 boat slips at pier. Rental boats, houseboats. 300 ft. of sand beach with bathhouse · picnic tables · grills · public launch · tennis and basketball courts. A handicapped-accessible fishing dock is located just off *STH 35*.

BU-9

LOCK & DAM #4 The observation tower, city boat landing (BU-10), public courtesy docks, and parking, are all accessible along the river below the corner of Main and Pine Streets.

The Great Alma Fishing Float provides easy access to excellent fishing below the Lock and Dam. A minimal fee includes pick-up at the dock. Some fishing gear is available. Breakfast and lunch are both served on the float.

A record-sized *gar* caught near Alma is displayed at the Hillcrest Motel at the north end of town. With the body of a northern pike and a long, narrow, toothy bill, it looks almost prehistoric and much different from the pencil-thin gar usually seen in fish displays. While 36 species of fish are commonly found in the Upper Mississippi River, an additional 70 species have been identified as rare or uncommon.

BU-11
BUENA VISTA PARK (Reach via *CTH E* from *STH 35* within city limits). Scenic view from top of 500-foot high bluff. Follow clearly marked signs from town for a good two miles. A unique view of the Lock & Dam system and dike directly below. Spectacular view of Upper and Lower Wiggle Waggle Sloughs and islands of the river. Watch young children! While this is a very lovely, well-developed park, there is no fencing at the lookout. Picnic tables·water·toilets

GREAT RIVER HARBOR AND CAMPGROUND (just south of Alma, *STH 35; river mile 747.9*). Full hook-up camping along the river with free dockage for campers. New amenities, boat docks, and slips. Miniature golf, cafe open 1991. Camp store·30-50-200 amp outlets·dump station·toilets·showers · houseboat rentals · cabin/trailer/boat rentals

---

SPECIAL EVENTS

Late MAY	Alma, *Park Festival* at Rieck's Lake Park.
Late SEPTEMBER	Alma, *Swiss Heritage Days*. Sponsored by the Alma Historical Society.
SEPTEMBER	*Alma Horse Pull.* *Backroads Tours* sponsored by the Buffalo County Historical Society.

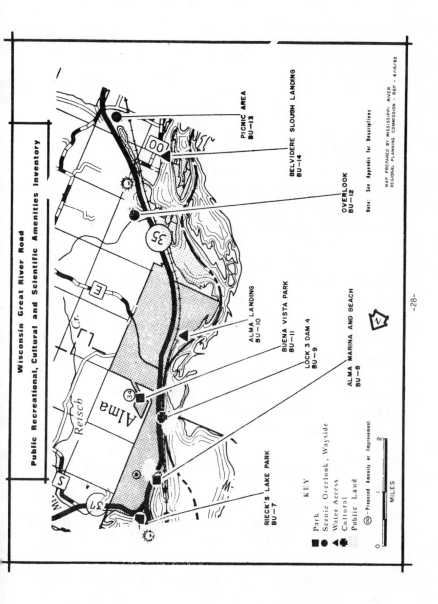

Wisconsin Great River Road

Public Recreational, Cultural and Scientific Amenities Inventory

PICNIC AREA
BU-13

BELVIDERE SLOUGH LANDING
BU-14

OVERLOOK
BU-12

ALMA LANDING
BU-10

BUENA VISTA PARK
BU-11

LOCK 3 DAM 4
BU-9

ALMA MARINA AND BEACH
BU-8

RIECK'S LAKE PARK
BU-7

Note: See Appendix for Descriptions

MAP PREPARED BY MISSISSIPPI RIVER
REGIONAL PLANNING COMMISSION - RGF - 6/15/82

KEY

■ Park
● Scenic Overlook, Wayside
▲ Water Access
✚ Cultural
 Public Land

∞ - Proposed Amenity or Improvement

MILES
0   1   2

LOGGING ON THE MISSISSIPPI

What may have been the largest log sorting and rafting works in the world once operated in a sluggish branch of the Chippewa River known as Beef (or Buffalo) Slough.

The Beef Slough sorting and rafting works was begun by a coalition of sawmill operators from down river and was supported by loggers and timberland owners who foresaw better prices if the logs could be sold on the open market. Until this time, the Chippewa River sawmill owners had a virtual monopoly on any logs that came down the Chippewa — and the Chippewa drained a third of the Wisconsin North Woods!

The Beef Slough Wars represented a determined effort by the Chippewa River mill owners to sabotage efforts by the Beef Slough group to ship logs through to the south. While they did not manage to halt the operation, the Chippewa mill owners did keep their competitor largely unprofitable until it was leased by Frederick Weyerhaeuser, a sawmill operator from Rock Island, IL. His *Mississippi Logging Company* provided the capital and expertise to end the war and change Wisconsin's logging from a local operation to an interstate industry.

Beef Slough provided a sheltered storage pond for logs floated downstream from northern logging camps on the Chippewa, Stillwater, Eau Claire and St. Croix rivers. Each log floated down these rivers was marked to identify the logger, its Beef Slough destination and even the sawmill for which it was destined further south. The marker's skills included determining which side of the log would float upward and to mark that side.

A hint for those who would accept the $20 challenge for balancing on a log in a lumberjack show: Ask to see that the log is floating naturally before you try to stand on it. There is a heavy side to every log and the log WILL roll so the heavy side is down.

Each log was tallied as it entered Beef Slough and sorted into the proper pocket for shipment. The logs were laid side by side until enough were collected to make a 50'x 500' raft called a *brail*. Each brail was then surrounded by a perimeter of logs with a hole drilled in the end of each log to receive a wooden plug which was connected by chain to another plug which went into the next log. Making the plugs was big business in itself, and a mill in Stoddard, WI, found an eager market when it began producing an all-wood plug that did not have to be removed when the logs arrived at the sawmill. Unfortunately, the forests ran out before Stoddard's plugs did.

Four to six brails were chained together to form a huge raft which was then pushed/guided by steamboats to the mills further downstream. Up to 12 steamboats a day were arriving and departing from the Slough during its busiest years, with rafts being stored in various sloughs and backwaters until pickup. More than 600 men were employed in the sorting, brailing and rafting works of the Mississippi Logging Company.

The sawmills to the south depended heavily on the Beef Slough operation for saw logs. Frederick Laue, in Alma, would buy rafts containing 6,000,000 board feet of saw logs. Sawed lumber was then rafted down river to lumberyards, such as those in La Crosse, which produced trim, planed lumber, moulding, and other wood products.

After the summer rafting season, many of the men spent the winter logging. Others, who logged all winter, worked farms they 'grubbed' out in the summer. During the winter, logs were piled on the riverbanks to await the spring thaw for shipping. Often, high water would scatter a portion of the harvest which was then eagerly retrieved not only by the loggers, but also by local farmers who built many of their buildings with such 'found' logs. Further south, sawed wood was similarly scattered.

In 1904, the last log raft was floated past Alma. Thirty years after the first loggers had arrived, there was no further sign of the lumber industry in Wisconsin. The 'inexhaustible' virgin forests of the north woods were gone. Today, of course, northern Wisconsin is again reforested and the lumber industries continue to be productive.

Much of this information is from **Alma on The Mississippi 1848-1932.** Compiled and Published by the Alma Historical Society, 1980. Beef Slough photo courtesy of the Area Research Center, UW-La Crosse

BU-13
PICNIC AREA

BU-14
BELVIDERE SLOUGH LANDING (*CTH 00* at Martin Subdivision). Hard Surface.

BUFFALO CITY is Wisconsin's smallest incorporated city. It is located along the Mississippi just off *STH 35* near Cochrane, and is known as the City of Parks, with seven public parks. Camping, motels, and a full-service marina are also located in town.

BU-15
BUFFALO LANDING (in City of Buffalo on Pomme de Terre *(Potato)* Slough, foot of Tenth Street).

BU-16
BUFFALO CITY PARK (between Tenth and Twelfth Streets). Picnic shelter • tables • grills

Sorting logs at Beef Slough.

BU-17
VILLAGE OF COCHRANE (west of *STH 35*). The Village of Cochrane was named for the first engineer to drive a train through the settlement. Like Stoddard, and the few other

villages not directly on the main channel of the river, the railroad brought new prosperity, industry and mobility — not to mention "standard time," schedules and other ties with the outside world.

The bluff which towers over the town was completely bald until recent times. Like most of the river valley, it was kept clear of trees and brush by grazing buffalo and then by domestic cattle and wild fires. An early local farmer who persisted in trying to graze cattle on the bluffside was often reminded that cows can't produce milk from rocks.

GOOSE LAKE MEMORIAL PARK (in village of Cochrane on Goose Lake — not part of the Mississippi River). A beautiful city park. Boat access is to this very small lake. No access to Mississippi River. Picnic tables • grills • shelter house • toilets • water • swimming pool • tennis courts

BU-18
LOWER SPRING LAKE LANDING (on Town Road on Spring Lake). Toilet • water • picnicking • boat ramp

BU-19
WHITMAN WILDLIFE ACCESS (Town Road on Slough well off *STH 35*). Primitive access on poor road to undeveloped ramp.

BU-20
MERRICK STATE PARK (on *STH 35,* approximately 7 miles south of Cochrane). Terrain varies from rugged 500 ' high sandstone bluffs to the lazy Mississippi and delicate marshland. Entry fee with additional camping fee. New RV campground with dump station. Several boat access launches. Excellent birding among islands, backwater areas. River's edge camping• fishing • swimming • picnicking • showers

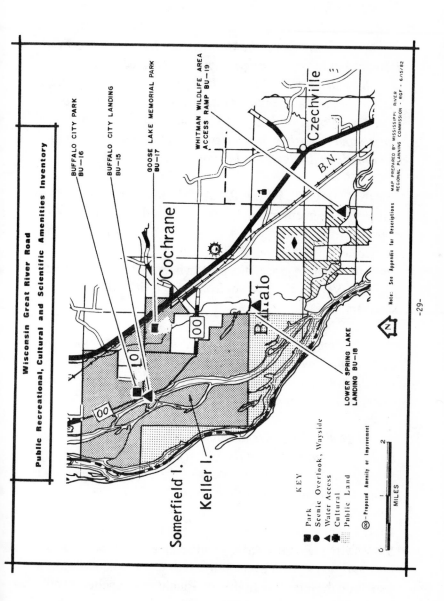

Wisconsin Great River Road

Public Recreational, Cultural and Scientific Amenities Inventory

BUFFALO CITY PARK
BU–16

BUFFALO CITY LANDING
BU–15

GOOSE LAKE MEMORIAL PARK
BU–17

WHITMAN WILDLIFE AREA
ACCESS RAMP BU–19

Czechville

B.N.

Cochrane

Buffalo

Note: See Appendix for Descriptions

LOWER SPRING LAKE
LANDING BU–18

Somerfield I.

Keller I.

KEY

Park
Scenic Overlook, Wayside
Water Access
Cultural
Public Land

⊗–Proposed Amenity or Improvement

MILES

MAP PREPARED BY MISSISSIPPI RIVER
REGIONAL PLANNING COMMISSION · RGF · 6/15/82

–29–

BU-21
UPPER FOUNTAIN CITY LANDING (north end of Fountain City). Small area, difficult to maneuver in.

Fountain City is the Maintenance Base for the St. Paul District Army Corps of Engineers. Many of the big work boats seen here are involved in the dredging operations, particularly to the north where constant dredging is required because of sediment brought in by the Chippewa River. Many of the large sandy beaches found between here and Prescott are man-made of dredged sand deposited by the Corps.

FOUNTAIN CITY HISTORICAL MARKER (on *STH 35*, in village). Commemorates the founding of the city in 1839 by a trader from Dubuque, IA. The town is named for the numerous springs in the bluffside. A landmark fountain and horse trough once graced the point where the two main streets join in a V. Excellent view from here of islands, river and sandbars.

Fountain City, often considered to be one of the most picturesque river towns along the Great River Road, is an excellent walking town with many interesting shops and riverside restaurants and cafes.

Notice the Swiss architecture on the Bank and other buildings, reminiscent of the largely Swiss heritage of early settlers. Several terraced, turn-of-the century homes and shops. The Golden Frog Restaurant overlooks the river.

BU-22
SWIMMING POOL PARK (south end of village on *STH 35*). On the right as you leave south end of town. The swimming pool is on the left of the highway. Picnic area • shelter • tennis courts • toilets

BU-23
LOWER FOUNTAIN CITY BOAT LANDING. South end of town.

BU-24
LOCK & DAM #5. Visitor observation platform. Privately operated fishing float in river downstream from dam. Good fishing along dam wall. Picnic tables • toilet • water

BU-25
BLUFF SIDING OVERLOOK AND PARK. Not located directly on the water. Parking site for fisherman's walk to river backwaters. Scenic view of river bottoms.

This tiny settlement was originally a railroad siding or parking area for trains going to/from Winona, MN. These pull-overs were needed when there was only one track rather than the two tracks which exist today. Winona's landmark Sugar Loaf Mountain is visible across the river.

STH 54 crosses west over the Main Channel of the river to Winona, MN.

BU-26
WINONA MUNICIPAL HARBOR *(STH 54,* 1 mile south of Bluff Siding). Private operator runs full service marina. Houseboat rentals • hard-surfaced boat launch • boat slips

BU-27
LATSCH ISLAND LANDING AND BEACH *(STH 54,* 1 mile south of Bluff Siding). Owned by the city of Winona, MN. Located in State of Wisconsin. Beach area. Hard surfaced boat ramp.

BU-20 — BU-23

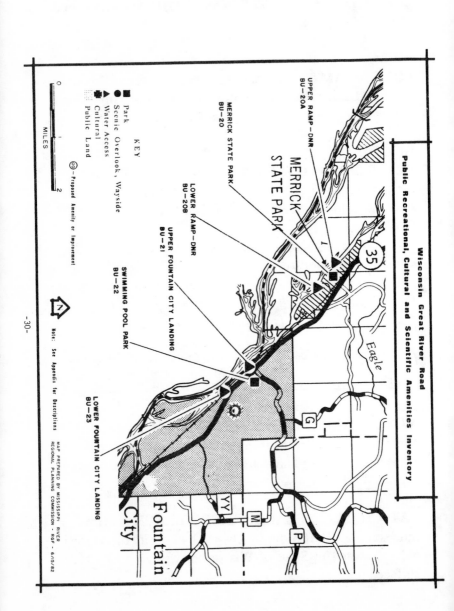

WINONA, MINNESOTA

A thriving lumber mill town during the last half of the 1800s, Winona today is in the forefront of the high-tech plastics industry. It is home to Watkins, Inc., the Winona Knitting Mills, St. Mary's College, and the oldest campus of the Minnesota State University System. James E. Fraser, of Winona, designed the Buffalo Nickel. The community was named for We-No-Nah, daughter of the Sioux Chief, Wa-Pah-Sha. The Winona Information Center is located just off *USH 14* on Huff St.

The *Polish Cultural Institute* offers displays of artifacts, heirlooms, and folk art brought to the area by Polish immigrants between 1857 and 1900. Golden-domed St. Stanislaus church, built in 1895 for the Polish-speaking congregation, seated 1800 people. *Polish Heritage Days* are held annually in May and commemorate the anniversary of the Polish consitution.

Zach's on the Tracks offers excellent dining with an old railroading flavor while the *Julius C. Wilkie Steamboat Center,* on the riverfront, serves lunch in the grand salon of a steamboat replica.

Five miles south, in the tiny village of Homer, is the historic *Bunnell House,* operated by the Winona County Historical Society. This gothic gem is the home of Willard Bunnell, the first permanent settler and last Indian trader in the Winona area. Bunnell's brother, Lafayette, was among the men who gave the name Yosemite to the National Park in California. The Winona County Historical Society also operates a large historical museum in downtown Winona and sponsors the *Victorian Fair* in October, a *Christmas House Tour* in December, and a themed quilt display in the spring.

BU-24 — BU-25

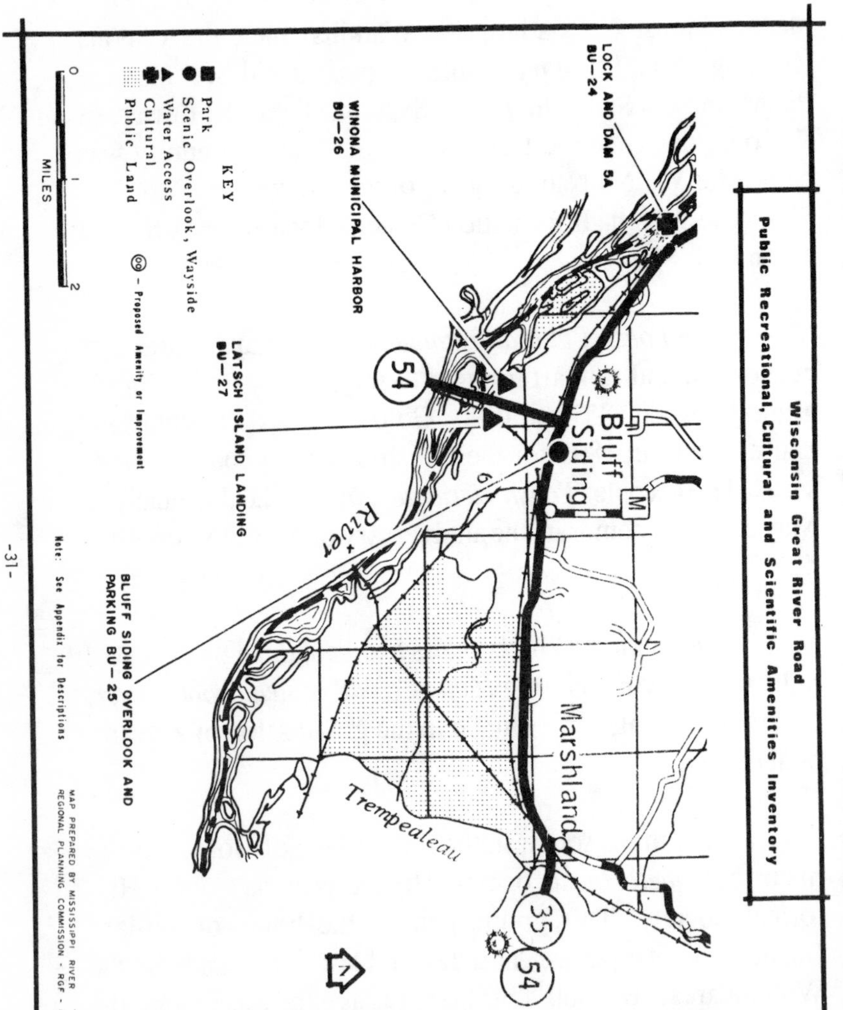
Wisconsin Great River Road
Public Recreational, Cultural and Scientific Amenities Inventory
LOCK AND DAM 5A
BU—24
WINONA MUNICIPAL HARBOR
BU—26
LATSCH ISLAND LANDING
BU—27
BLUFF SIDING OVERLOOK AND
PARKING BU—25
Bluff
Siding
Marshland
River
Trempealeau
54
35
M
7
KEY
Park
Scenic Overlook, Wayside
Water Access
Cultural
Public Land
– Proposed Amenity or Improvement
0
1
2
MILES
Note: See Appendix for Descriptions
MAP PREPARED BY MISSISSIPPI RIVER
REGIONAL PLANNING COMMISSION - RGF - 6/15/82

The 'True' Garden of Eden

TREMPEALEAU COUNTY

Trempealeau is the only town found along the Great River Road in Trempealeau County. In spite of French dominance during the early fur trading days, Trempealeau and Prairie du Chien are the only river towns whose early settlement was decidedly French (Canadian).

Several portions of the neighboring town of *Galesville* are on the National Register of Historic Places. Although Galesville's unique town square is worth a visit in itself, the drive to Galesville gives the traveler a first-hand view of the entire 'Garden of Eden' and the great circle of bluffs which cradles the area from north of Trempealeau, west to Galesville, and then south to meet the river again just below La Crosse. *STH 93* from Trempealeau to *USH 53* crosses extensive bottomlands, crisscrossed by rivers, streams and even lakes. A broad prairie scoured by the restless meanderings of the ancient Black and Mississippi rivers stretches from Galesville to La Crosse.

The Garden of Eden Story Retold

It was over 100 years ago that a Galesville pastor became convinced that the well-watered Trempealeau plain, not Asia, was the true site of Eden's Garden. His theory is presented in the booklet, *Garden of Eden,* reprints of which are available from some county businesses.

Among Rev. Slyke's arguments is the simple fact that no other habitable spot has been discovered which conforms as well to the description of the Garden of Eden in Genesis 2:8-14. That is, a rich agricultural area located on the *east* bank of a *great river* in the middle of the country of Eden. According to Genesis, three smaller rivers must flow from the Great River to water the Garden. As Rev. Slyke observed, the Trempealeau, Black, and La Crosse rivers all emptied into the Mississippi through Trempealeau County.

Many more comparisons are drawn including the fact that its original inhabitants dressed first in aprons then in furs, indicating a temperate climate. And the area has its serpents-- rattlesnakes are abundant in the natural hanging gardens, the grand circle of bluffs which shelter the plain.

In his booklet, Slyke challenges the world to prove him wrong in his deductions. To date, no one has.

SPECIAL EVENTS

Early
JULY

Catfish Days, village of Trempealeau. Enjoy fresh catfish, live music, entertainment, food and beverages.

Early
OCTOBER

Apple Affair, Galesville town square. The annual festival features homemade apple desserts, crafts, antiques and live music. A popular bike tour winds through all the orchards. Bus tours of the orchards are also available.

Tour Route: Trempealeau to Galesville

TE-1

OLD SCHOOL SITE PICNIC AREA (south side of *STH 35-54,* 3-1/4 miles west of Centerville, across from cemetery). Not on waterfront • hand pump for water • no camping

TE-2

TREMPEALEAU NATIONAL WILDLIFE REFUGE (map symbol indicates headquarters location. Refuge is located east of Marshland between the old Chicago Northwestern right-of-way and the Mississippi River). Turn-off is clearly marked on *STH 35*. A must-visit refuge for birders and others interested in Mississippi River wildlife. River access for canoers. Hiking, biking permitted on service roads. Toilets • water • parking • no specific picnic area

Within the refuge, follow the 4-1/2 mile circle drive. Pick up pamphlet with self-guided tour from the display at the beginning of the circle. In the forested portion, look for hawks, ruffed grouse, cuckoos, owls, yellow-breasted chat and bluebirds. In marshes, look for grebes, rare double-crested cormorants, bitterns, geese, ducks and osprey, all of which nest in the refuge. Red-shouldered hawks, bald eagles and white-tailed deer may also be seen. The best time for wildlife viewing is early morning and late afternoon.

5 Miles to Perrot State Park.

TREMPEALEAU, WISCONSIN

As is so often the case along the river, this small town holds many surprises. The historic *Trempealeau Hotel* offers Bed (needed hotel restorations are in progress) and leisurely Breakfast with a terrific view of this narrow stretch of river and the scenic Minnesota bluffs. Try a tasty homemade Belgian waffle as a breakfast treat. Reservations are suggested for weekend visits. There are two modern motels in town.

The short Main Street is included in the National Register of Historic Places as an historic commercial district. The brick buildings date from the 1890's. The town's business district originally stretched for two blocks along the riverfront, with warehouses built out over the water for easy loading by both steamboats and freight trains. Only the Hotel survived the fire of 1888 which destroyed the rest of the two-block business district. The building was moved to its present spot by teams of horses.

Several craftspersons are restoring the old buildings on Hill Street. The *Moonshadow Art Glass Shop* offers traditional cut glass arts and a newer fused glass technique. *Italianate Antiques* is located in an 1850's home on *STH 93* on the east entrance into town.

Geography

Geologists have suggested that before the last glacial period, the main channel of the Mississippi ran through the five-mile-wide valley between Perrot Park and the Galesville bluffs. Trempealeau Mountain stood by itself at the mouth of the Trempealeau River. In the great rush of glacial melting, the huge quantity of gravel and silt carried by the river eventually blocked the old channel. The river then eroded its way through the bluffs north of Trempealeau Mountain in order to flow in its present valley south and west of Perrot Park.

A Bit of Trempealeau History
(From: Trempealeau Historical Album, 1867-1967)

It has been told that as early as 1731 Swiss missionaries were at Trempealeau and, around 1820, there was a fur trading camp at Trempealeau Mountain. But not until 1836 was there any attempt at permanent settlement in the area.

In 1837, Hercules Dousman (builder of Villa Louis in Prairie du Chien), representing the American Fur Company of Prairie du Chien, sent two representatives to the area to establish a woodyard on the island opposite the current site of Trempealeau. John Doville remained to become the first white farmer in Trempealeau County.

The town was an inland gateway, via Beaver Creek and the Trempealeau and Black river valleys. Deer, elk, bear, wolves, cougar and other fur bearing animals were plentiful at this time.

Many of the settlers were French-Canadians with such names as Rosseau, Boulte, Goulet, and Grignon. By 1846, there were half a dozen log cabins scattered along the riverfront, occupied by French and French-Canadian families. Between 1852 and 1856, the name of the village alternated several times between *Montaville* and *Trempealeau*. The latter has held since 1856. The only other township in

Trempealeau county in 1852 was the town of *Gale*. When the first county election was held in that year, Montaville cast 37 votes. The town of Gale, 20 votes.

Trempealeau was a lively place during wheat times. Farmers throughout the county brought grain in for milling and shipment. River traffic opened in 1857. The Chicago Northwestern Railroad was finished in 1871 and wheat shipments increased from 1000 bushels of wheat to 5000 bushels per day. Six passenger trains a day stopped in the village. Another train made several trips a day from Galesville to Trempealeau. The round trip ticket was 32 cents.

By 1918 the railroad was suffering from competition with the automobile and by 1922 passenger service was discontinued. Today, only the Burlington Northern freight trains roar through town.

> **From the Trempealeau Hotel travel 3-1/2 miles west on First Street to PERROT STATE PARK.**

Excellent views of the riverside bluffs as one travels west (up-river) toward the park. 1st Peak (Liberty Peak) with the flag pole and 2nd Peak (Eagle Cliff) above the old village park with its boldly differentiated limestone and sandstone strata. The 3rd bluff is named after the Brunnel brothers. The 4th major bluff is Brady's Bluff, just above the entrance to the park.

The stone remains of the *Melchoir Brewery and Riverfront Hotel* are still visible along First Street. Three large caves which opened onto the hillside behind the brewery provided storage at a constant 44-degrees for newly brewed beer. Melchoir's Lager Beer made Trempealeau famous long before Schlitz made Milwaukee famous. The brewery contained a bar room, dance hall, family residence, and 16 guest rooms. By the late 1860's, Melchoir's was well known throughout the territory.

ED SULLIVAN'S RESTAURANT offers fine dining on the river, an Irish gift shop, and displays of original portraits by artist John Solie, whose work often appears in *Readers Digest,* and on record jackets and book jackets.

TE-3
PERROT STATE PARK. Historical marker commemorates the 1685 trading post of the French explorer, Nicholas Perrot. Hopwellian Indian burial mounds • naturalist programs • fishing • deer hunting in season (muzzle loaders only) • boat landing • hiking trails (with interpretive pamphlet for Brady Bluff Trail) • swimming • picnicking • hiking • scenic bluffs • riverviews

Excellent *camping* area with 97 sites. *Winter camping* with 8-1/2 miles of groomed, graded cross country ski trails. Electricity • dump station • playgrounds • flush toilets

TREMPEALEAU MOUNTAIN

This traditional landmark is visible from the swimming/camping area in the park and is unusual in that it is one of only three solid rock islands found along the full length of the river which is as high as the surrounding bluffs. It is the only 'bluff' the full length of the river that is surrounded by water. This made it an important navigational guide for early steamboat pilots.

Early Indians believed that Trempealeau Mountain had been carried off by supernatural forces from the neighborhood of the Sioux Village on the site of modern Winona. The Sioux called it the "moved mountain."

The Winnebagoes called it "the mountain whose foot is bathed in water." Its height made it a prominent landmark for Indian gatherings and its watery 'moat' protected it from wild fires which were frequent on the prairie. As a result, Trempealeau Mountain has a long history as an Indian ceremonial ground. Local folklore suggests that an Indian 'dugout' canoe can be found at the very top of the mountain.

The French called it "La Montagne qui trempe a l'eau" — or the mountain steeped in water. At the time of the French fur traders, the mountain was surrounded by a large bay formed at the mouth of the Trempealeau River.

The grasses and sandbars which clog the bay surrounding the 425' high mountain are clear evidence of the increasing sedimentation that plagues much of the river. Tons of sediment is carried by the river and wherever the current slows, sediment will settle, filling in sloughs and backwater areas. The problem is aggravated by the lock and dam system which has substantially slowed the flow of the river by dividing it into a chain of 'pools.'

Return to the Village of Trempealeau

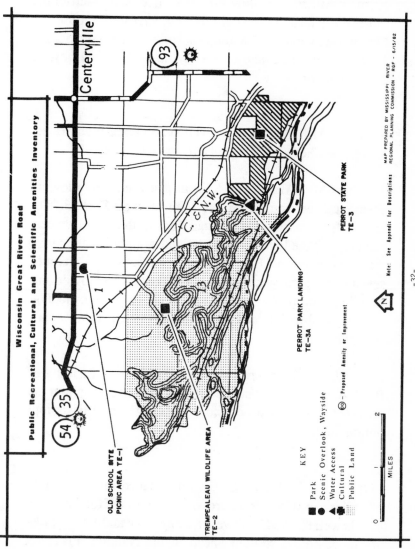

Wisconsin Great River Road

Public Recreational, Cultural and Scientific Amenities Inventory

Centerville

OLD SCHOOL SITE
PICNIC AREA TE-1

TREMPEALEAU WILDLIFE AREA
TE-2

PERROT PARK LANDING
TE-3A

PERROT STATE PARK
TE-3

KEY

Park

Scenic Overlook, Wayside

Water Access

Cultural

Public Land

– Proposed Amenity or Improvement

Note: See Appendix for Descriptions

MAP PREPARED BY MISSISSIPPI RIVER
REGIONAL PLANNING COMMISSION – RGF – 6/15/82

MILES

-32-

TE-4
LOCK AND DAM #6 (southeast end of Village of Trempealeau. Follow *STH 93* east to the Mini-Mart on the Corner of Fremont Street. Follow Fremont Street south across the railroad tracks and veer right to the river.) Visitor observations area to view lock operations. Toilet • water • picnicking *Fishing float access near east end of the Lock & Dam, beyond Chet's Landing.*

TE-5
TREMPEALEAU BOAT LANDING (in Lock & Dam area, to west of Chet's Landing). Hard surface ramp.

THE TREMPEALEAU LAKES are also found by following Fremont Street south from the Mini-Mart on *STH 93*. Directly after crossing the railroad tracks, the traveler veers right to visit the lock & dam area, and straight ahead to visit the lakes noted in TE-7. The lakes are actually a chain of seven small, picturesque, spring-fed lakes which provide outstanding fishing (everything but walleye) and canoeing. Several well-maintained boat landings and parking areas, shelterhouse.

Rental cottages and *camping* at Larry's Landing or Birch Acres. Notice that the cabins scattered throughout the area are on *stilts* due to occasional flooding in this Mississippi bottomland.

TE-6
LONG LAKE LANDING. Gravel surfaced ramp about 1-1/2 miles from the railroad crossing, the turn-off for the Lakes area is well marked. However, *Long Lake* and *Round Lake* are to be found straight ahead in the National Fish and Wildlife Refuge. They are not marked.

BIRCH ACRES COTTAGES AND CAMPING is located on spring-fed Round Lake. Due to flooding since construction of the lock & dam system, Long Lake is now largely a backwater slough. Past Birch Acres, the road deteriorates into a dead-end dirt path well inside the refuge. It is a convenient access to wilderness bottomland.

TE-7, TE-8
TREMPEALEAU LAKE PUBLIC HUNTING AND FISH-ING AREA. Public hunting and fishing grounds in the Trempealeau Lakes area. Three well-maintained hard surface boat landings. (Map available at Birch Acres). Fishing on all lakes (First, Second, Third, and Mud Lake) is very good. February ice fishing derby is held on Third Lake.

Return to Fremont Street and *STH 93*, east.

Leave Trempealeau on *STH 93*, east.
8 miles to junction with *USH 53/STH 35*.

Just outside the Trempealeau village limits, is the *Great River Trail* providing biking, hiking, and snowmobiling along the old Chicago and Northwestern railroad bed. The path continues through town and around Brady Bluff to the north entrance of Perrot Park.

LA-1
BOAT LANDING (south side of *STH 93*, east of Black River, at bridge). Large landing on the Black River. Good birding, canoeing area.

12 miles to City of La Crosse.

TE-4 — TE-8

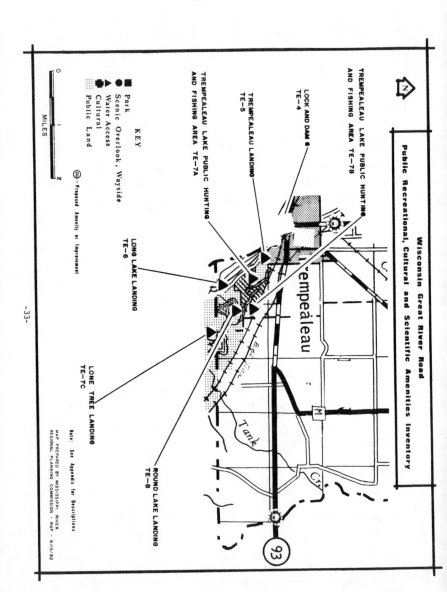

VAN LOON WILDLIFE AREA (located north and south of *STH 93* along the Black River). 6-1/2 square miles of public hunting and recreation land. Also known as the McGilvary Bottoms, after the first white settler in the area, a Scot who purchased the land in 1852.

A 1-3/4 mile trail called *Seven-Bridges Road* allows the hiker convenient access to the wildlife area. Turn north from *STH 93* onto *CTH XX* at the top of the large rise after crossing the Black River. Access to the trail is about 1-1/2 miles ahead on the left side. The DNR sign is fairly well hidden at the entry, so watch your odometer. The trail includes seven 17-foot-wide bridges built between 1891 and 1892. Visitors will be treated to brilliant leaf colors in the fall and plentiful wildflowers in the spring. Excellent birding, cross-country skiing, and hunting access.

The turn onto *CTH XX* is a good spot to stop for a moment of *geology watching*. The entire range of bluffs, from Trempealeau to Holmen, is clearly seen from this point, sweeping in a great semi-circle to the north and back around to Perrot Park. On a clear day, the traveler may be able to find the landmark bluffs in Trempealeau — 1st Peak, 2nd Peak, Brady's Bluff and Trempealeau Mountain. This protective circle of bluffs has contributed to the success of apple orchards in the Galesville area and to the hypothesis that this valley is, in fact, the Garden of Eden.

LA-2
GREAT RIVER ROAD HISTORICAL MARKER (Jct. of *STH 93* and *STH 35/USH 53*). Historical Marker describes the establishment of the Mississippi River Parkway - Great River Road System. Picnic table.

THE BLACK RIVER

Like the Mississippi, the Black River has been flooding and wandering erratically over the valley floor since the ice ages. It began as an outlet for glacial Lake Wisconsin, which covered much of central Wisconsin.

Early settlers found little use for these bottomlands except hunting and lumbering. It is estimated that during the last half of the 19th century more than 5 billion board feet of logs and lumber were floated through this area from the pine forests up-river. Black River logging may have been the single most important element in the early prosperity of the city of La Crosse. The source of the Black River today is Hulls Lake, north and east of Eau Claire. It empties into the Mississippi at Lake Onalaska, just down river from Trempealeau.

The area is now used primarily for public duck and deer hunting or fishing. Squirrels, raccoon and ruffed grouse are abundant. Trapping, hiking, and bird and wildflower study are popular. An *overnight camping* area for canoeists can be found along the south bank of the river, about two-thirds of a mile downstream from the bridge on *USH 53*.

Alternate Route
GALESVILLE, WISCONSIN SIDE TRIP
Follow *USH 53 /35* north to Galesville.

Though located about eight miles off the Great River Road, Galesville's unique town square and scenic setting merits a visit by the traveler with time to stop.

Drugan's Castle Mound Golf Course and Restaurant is located along the highway, as is *SANDMAN'S RV RESORT* and the *POW WOW CAMPGROUND RESORT* with facilities for swimming, mini-golf, and other recreational activities.

DECORAH'S PEAK is a rocky knob perched atop a bluff which becomes visible directly ahead, on *USH 53*. The Historical Marker describing the significance of the peak is located along *USH 53* as the road curves around the bluff. The flat plain traversed by *USH 53/STH 35* between La Crosse and Galesville, was once the site of a great Winnebago Indian village ruled by chief Decorah. At the foot of the Decorah Peak Bluff, one of the bloodiest Indian battles in history was waged between raiding Chippewas and the more peaceful Winnebagoes. The Winnebago village was ruined. Decorah's warriors were wiped out. Decorah, himself wounded, was able to escape to the rocky peak.

Later that night he was able to slip away down the Black River to the Mississippi where more of his band was camped. With these reinforcements, Decorah again attacked the Chippewas who were in the midst of their victory celebrations. This time the Winnebagoes won the battle. Decorah lived until the days of the white settlers, when his history of the battle was recorded.

Decorah's main claim to fame (as far as the white settlers were concerned) was that he accompanied the Sac chief, Black Hawk, when he surrendered to army forces at Ft. Crawford in Prairie du Chien. Legend is that Decorah ran 90 miles in one day to notify officials at Ft. Crawford when he saw Black Hawk passing through the valley from atop his rocky look-out.

GALESVILLE, WISCONSIN

The city of Galesville is located along the Beaver Creek bluffs and the banks of Lake Marinuka. It was established in 1853 by George Gale, who decided to found his own town and university after he was unable to convince the people of La Crosse to establish a college in that community. His *Gale College* buildings now house the *Marynook* ecumenically oriented retreat center.

A.A. ARNOLD'S EASTSIDE FARM is located off *USH 53* on the north end of town, east of Skogen's IGA. The 15-room Italianate house is on the National Register of Historic Places and is being restored. The home's three-story-high tower houses a beautiful spiral staircase which leads to four arched windows offering a broad view in all four directions. The estate of the Yankee-lawyer-turned-gentleman-farmer originally consisted of 400 acres and a rare 50x50 foot New York style barn with an indoor silo — the first upright silo built in the United States.

Lake Marinuka is named for an Indian Princess buried at the north end of the lake in 1884. Several grand old homes line its shores. Turn left at the *Town Square* for a view of Lake Marinuka and the *Ridge Avenue Residential District* which, like the Town Square, is on the National Register of Historic Places.

Historic Queen Anne-style homes overlook the lovely Cance Memorial City Park at 6th and Ridge Ave. Continue along Ridge Avenue until 12th Street. Follow 12th Street to the Marynook complex.

Sacia Home on Ridge Avenue

BEAVER CREEK, which runs along the cliffs on the south-east side of town, provided power for the town's early sawmill and flour mill. *CTH K,* directly after the bridge into town, leads down along Beaver Creek before sweeping back up the hill to the *Historic Town Square* and *Gazebo.* Main Street Antiques, a co-op of 10 dealers, is located in a restored building on the square. Bean Pot Antiques is located north of town on *STH 53.*

The *Millroad Cafe and Common Market* are unique spots to visit, ideal for a relaxing lunch with scenic overlook of Beaver Creek and its gorge. Quality entertainment on weekends. Reservations suggested for dinner (served week-ends only).

Access to *High Cliff Park* (est. 1868) and its unusual swinging footbridge is just west of the cafe. A short scenic walk over the swinging bridge and along the cliffs leads to a spring-fed pool. The path continues along the creek then past the dam which was originally built to provide power for the grain mill located opposite (thus, Mill Road.) The green tint of Beaver Creek develops as its feeder springs trickle through the limestone of neighboring bluffs.

**Return south on *USH 53/STH 35* to La Crosse County.
8 miles to Holmen.**

Backwater area on the Mississippi, painting by Marion Biehn.

Crossroads

LA CROSSE COUNTY

The county of La Crosse lies divided between the broad prairie lowlands and the agriculture rich bluff tops. The principal cities of Holmen, Onalaska, La Crosse and West Salem are among the few river towns which have prospered and grown during the past 100 years. Agriculture, diversified manufacturing, education, and tourism have all contributed to the economic well-being of the area.

Three large rivers converge on the city of La Crosse as does I-90 and several major highways and railways. Before the coming of the Europeans, the area was a gathering place of Indians for games and trading. Arrowheads and other relics are often found in the area. Indian folklore holds that a tornado will never occur in an area where three rivers meet and, to date, this has held true for the City of La Crosse.

> ## Tour Route: Holmen to La Crosse on *STH 35*

(LA-3 through LA-8, below, are all located off *STH 35* on Brice Prairie, just north and west of the city of Onalaska, WI.

LA-3
HUNTERS WALK-IN ACCESS. Primarily used by duck hunters.

SPECIAL EVENTS

JULY 4th — *Riverfest,* La Crosse Riverside Park. Six days of continuous free family entertainment. Live events all day, Venetian Parade of Lights, special food tent, symphony concert, fireworks display.

Mid-JULY — *La Crosse Interstate Fair,* West Salem fairgrounds.

Late JULY — *Art Fair on the Green,* UW-La Crosse Campus Mall. Exhibits and sales by artists in various media, including painting, pottery, weaving, jewelry, photography.

Late AUGUST — *Holmen Kornfest,* Holmen, WI. Parade, softball tournament and tons of fresh, hot, buttered corn-on-the-cob.

SEPTEMBER Labor Day Weekend — *Great River Traditional Music and Crafts Festival,* UW-La Crosse Campus Mall. Extensive displays and sales of traditional crafts. Musicians, storytellers, artisans.

Mid-SEPTEMBER — *Applefest* in La Crescent, MN. Parade, arts, crafts, food and beverage sales, live musical entertainment, rides.

Last weekend in SEPTEMBER through first week of October. — *OKTOBERFEST,* north and southside Fest grounds in La Crosse. Nationally known and considered to be the largest in the midwest. Carnival, food & beverage tents, Miss La Crosse/Oktoberfest contest, button collecting, Maple Leaf Parade on Saturday morning is 3-4 hours long. Several special events throughout the week. Fest ends with the Torchlight Parade on Thursday evening.

LA-4
LAKE ONALASKA UPPER BRICE PRAIRIE LANDING.
Hard surface ramp.

LA-5
SWARTHOUT PARK (across *CTH ZB* from LA-4). Play
ground • picnicking • toilets • water

LA-6
HOLMEN SQUARE (north end of village of Holmen, along
STH 35). Convenient shopping area provides several depart-
ment stores • cafe • groceries • restaurant • gasoline

FMB TRAILER SALES AND SERVICE (along *STH 35*, just south
of Holmen Square shopping area). Complete recreational
vehicle sales • service • parts and supplies

HOLMEN COUNTY PARK (south side of village, adjacent
to village park). Halfway Creek ravine and picturesque foot
bridge. Pleasant rest stop offers picnic sites, shelter, and
hiking trails.

LA-7
HOLMEN MIDDLE SCHOOL PARK.

BRICE PRAIRIE LOOP

This side trip wanders through the large prairie low-
land between the highway and Lake Onalaska. Follow *CTH
OT* which dips into the tiny burg of *Midway* (between
Onalaska and Holmen). Once a stop on the Chicago and
Northwestern rail line, Midway boasted three churches, a lum-

beryard, a saloon, a feed mill, stockyard and grocery store (only the grocery store and saloon are still there). The *Great River Bike Trail* runs through town along the old rail bed.

Archaeological excavations have been on-going in the Midway area since 1919. The excavations have yielded a wealth of information and artifacts pertaining to the lifeways of the *Oneta* Indians who lived and farmed on this prairie 500 years ago. In 1978 the *Midway Village Site* was placed on the National Register of Historic Places. It is considered to be one of the most valuable prehistoric sites on the Upper Mississippi.

The *Mississippi Valley Archaeological Center* is actively excavating several sites in the La Crosse area. Call 608-785-8463 if you are interested in participating in an archaeological dig.

Follow *CTH ZN* out of Midway. After crossing the railroad tracks, begin watching for the Bison herd of the *Circle D Buffalo Ranch,* which is considered to be one of the most successful bison ranches in the nation. These are not *'beefalo,'* but about 300 pure *American Bison*. While they may appear quite docile in their pens, bison can not be domesticated. Were the fences not electric, even the calves could easily walk right through the sturdiest corrals.

Reconstructed ceramic pot from Midway excavations.

The main feed lot is near the farmhouse at the junction with *CTH Z*. As many as 70 of the 2-1/2 year old bulls are held in the feed lot until butchering. 70 animals will consume 2400 pounds of hay and 10,000 lbs of grain a week — which is actually less than 70 cows would eat.

There are approximately 80,000 bison in America today. In comparison, 80,000 head of cattle are slaughtered each **day** in this country. The buffalo meat is tasty and is butchered and prepared exactly as is beef. *Circle D* buffalo meat can be purchased locally either at the Holmen locker plant where it is butchered or at *Marge's Riverview Restaurant and Lounge,* on *STH 53* in Onalaska, where it is prepared.

Continuing following *CTH Z* to the north as it meets Lake Onalaska to find LA-3 through LA-5. Turn east onto *CTH Z* to return to *STH 35* and LA-8.

RED SAILS RESORT AND CAMPGROUND (located on *CTH Z* just west of *STH 35*). Motel and camping accommodations. Scenic lake watching opportunities from outdoor deck and resort tavern. Public may use concrete boat landing, free. Electricity • laundromat • dump station • canoe and fishing boat rentals

According to the DNR, Lake Onalaska *(Pool 7)* has more fish caught per individual than any other pool on the Mississippi; thus Onalaska's logo, *Sunfish Capital of the World.*

'Pool' is the term applied to the broad lake-like areas that occur in the river just north of the dams. Lake Onalaska and Lake Pepin are just such wide spots in the river.

LA-1 — LA-7

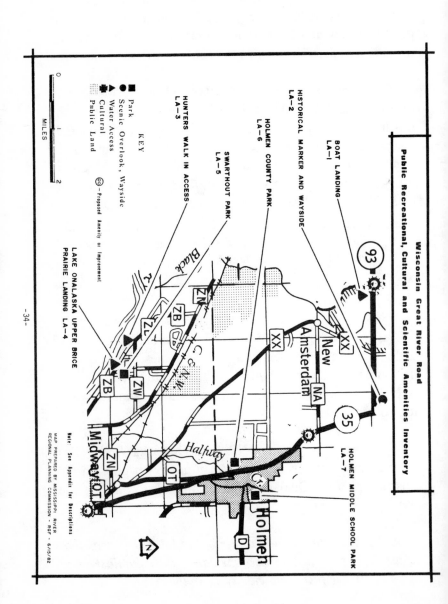

LA-8

MOSEY PUBLIC BOAT LANDING (West on *CTH Z* less than 1/2 mile.) Provides access to Lake Onalaska. Steep, hard surface ramp with fisherman parking. *Schafer Boat Livery* adjacent to the landing, offers boat and motor rentals and bait. Antique shop is located just beyond the boat landing.

THE GREAT RIVER TRAIL ACCESS is located right off *STH 35* on *CTH Z*. Biking, hiking, cross-country skiing on the old Chicago and Northwestern rail bed.

LA-9

FISHERMAN PARKING. Located just behind Marge's Restaurant on *STH 35*. Turn right and then left. Large parking area. No boat ramp. Stairs to river across railroad track.

Marge's Restaurant and Lounge (just north of waysides LA-10, LA-9). Complete menu of award-winning buffalo dinners, as well as usual restaurant fare with unusually good view of Lake Onalaska.

HOVE'S CAMPING. Across the street from Marge's Restaurant. RV sales • service • parts and supplies

LA-10

SCENIC RIVER OVERLOOK. Descriptive marker for history of Upper Mississippi River National Wildlife and Fish Refuge. Picnicking • no toilets • no water

LA-11

SCENIC OVERLOOK of Lake Onalaska. The airport runways are visible on French Island. Good fishing off the dike visible on far left of lake. Picnicking • water • no toilet

INSIGHT

MARILYN HURT, MAYOR
CITY OF DAKOTA, MINNESOTA
(Population 360)

If I had to pick one thought to relay about life on the Mississippi, it is this: the single most important thing we can do in the Upper Midwest is to clean up the river. The Clean Water Act passed by the 99th Congress is probably the most important legislation of that year for our area. It should help St. Paul get its water treatment plants modernized. This part of the river is already so much cleaner than it is down river. We have a responsibility to maintain it. All of our livelihoods up and down the river rely on a clean Mississippi, a safe environment for man and wildlife.

ONALASKA, WISCONSIN

The name *Onalaska* was chosen by its founder, Thomas G. Rowe in 1851 after a favorite poem that included a verse which spoke of "Oonalaska's shore." Thus, while many river towns have names of Indian or French origin, Onalaska is Russian or Aleution. At the time, the only other similarly named town was Unalaska, a village in the Aleution Islands. Today, there is an Onalaska in Washington and one in Texas. *(from Myer Katz, Echos of our Past)*

A Bit of Onalaska History

The town has a vibrant past that is quite separate from that of La Crosse. The town site was purchased by a young man from New York, about 10 years after La Crosse had begun to prosper. The first business was a tavern for rivermen.

Lumbering was the significant industry during the first 50 years in Onalaska. Over 6 billion board feet of white pine floated down the Black River through Onalaska during that time. In 1893 there were 4,400 men employed in lumbering as sorters, loggers, raftsmen, towboat workers, and in the shingle mills. Many of them came from Canada, Maine, and Norway, where they had lumbering experience. At different times, 33 sawmills operated between Onalaska and La Crosse. Saloons, hotels, supply stores and four different railroads grew up to service the lumbering industry.

With the decline in lumbering, the railroads and many of the businesses left town. Today, 75% of the population is employed in La Crosse, though there are several local industries. The population has doubled since 1970 to near 10,000 people, making Onalaska one of the largest towns along the Wisconsin shore.

LA-12 ONALASKA COUNTY PARK (east of *USH 53* in city of Onalaska). Not on river • three shelter houses • picnicking • playground

French Island is located just west of Onalaska. The Mississippi River runs along its western shore, the Black River between the island and Onalaska. At one time, the Island was aptly named for its numerous French-Canadian occupants. The La Crosse Municipal Airport is located here.

LA-13
LOUIS NELSON COUNTY PARK (located at the north end of Lake Shore Drive on French Island, adjacent to the *La Crosse Sailing Club*). Picnicking • water • toilets • gravel boat ramp

LA-14, 15, 16, 17
Numerous public boat landings on the perimeter of French Island provide access to Lake Onalaska and the Black River.

LA-18
CAMPBELL BEACH (on Fisherman's Road, east of La Crosse Airport). Sand beach.

LA-19
NATIONAL FISHERY RESEARCH LAB (2630 Fanta Reed Rd., along eastern shore of French Island). The Lab conducts research on methods of controlling non-game fish species and their impact on sport and commercial fishing.

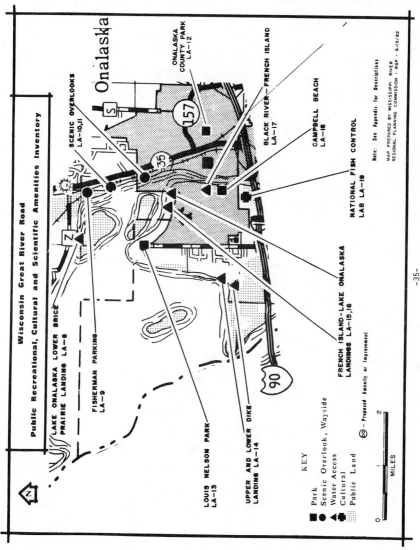

Wisconsin Great River Road
Public Recreational, Cultural and Scientific Amenities Inventory

Onalaska

LAKE ONALASKA LOWER BRICE
PRAIRIE LANDING LA-8

FISHERMAN PARKING
LA-9

SCENIC OVERLOOKS
LA-10,11

ONALASKA
COUNTY PARK
LA-12

BLACK RIVER—FRENCH ISLAND
LA-17

CAMPBELL BEACH
LA-18

NATIONAL FISH CONTROL
LAB LA-19

LOUIS NELSON PARK
LA-13

UPPER AND LOWER DIKE
LANDING LA-14

FRENCH ISLAND-LAKE ONALASKA
LANDINGS LA-15,16

Note: See Appendix for Descriptions

MAP PREPARED BY MISSISSIPPI RIVER
REGIONAL PLANNING COMMISSION - RGF - 6/15/82

KEY

■ Park
● Scenic Overlook, Wayside
▲ Water Access
✚ Cultural
░ Public Land
50 - Proposed Amenity or Improvement

0   1   2
MILES

-35-

BRIDGEVIEW MALL SHOPPING AREA is located along *STH 35*.
Discount store • fast food • groceries • gas

U-HAUL RV PARTS AND SERVICES located just south of
Bridgeview Mall.

LA-20, LA-22
Several *boat ramps* are located along the Black River just
north of downtown La Crosse. The LOGAN STREET LANDING
(LA-20) is a hard surface ramp. The CLINTON STREET BOAT
LANDING (LA-22) has been recently resurfaced and enlarged.

LA-21
The BLACK RIVER BEACH (North Side). Bathhouse •
concession stand • playground

LA-23
COPELAND PARK is a major La Crosse City Park and the
Northside Oktoberfest grounds. Located north of the
central business district. Wading pool • tennis, baseball and
basketball courts • picnicking • covered ice skating and
hockey rink • toilets • water

*The numerous cottages extending from the shoreline
into the water at Copeland Park are officially 'boat houses'
which are protected from eviction by long-term leases from
the city. The DNR regulates any further construction or renovation of the boathouses with the intention that they will
gradually be phased out.*

LA CROSSE, WISCONSIN

La Crosse is by far the largest city located in the river valley. Many of the old familiar food and lodging chains are again abundantly available. A quick list of must-do's while in La Crosse includes a look at the 'castles' on Cass Street; the view from Grandad Bluff; a visit to Riverside Park and its *Riverside, USA* display, and a cruise on a paddlewheeler. Valley View Mall on *USH 16* offers Dayton's, Penny's, and Sears. Some may be interested in touring the *Hixon House* or the *G. Heileman Brewery*.

A Brief History of La Crosse

The name, La Crosse, originated long before the town was established. The French fur traders referred to this broad treeless prairie as *Prairie La Crosse* for the game of *la crosse* which is similar to games the French saw Indians playing in the area.

The first settler in the La Crosse area was one Nathan Myrick who at age 19 left his home in Westport, NY, to settle on the Mississippi. He built the first log cabin near the present site of Spence Park, at the foot of State Street. Just to the north of his home he established the first trading post. Myrick stayed in the area for eight years before moving to St. Paul.

Strategically located half-way between Galena, IL, and St. Paul, and blessed with great scenic beauty and adequate space beneath the bluffs to support a good-sized community, Myrick's fledgling village prospered.

In 1858, La Crosse was the major steamboat port south of St. Paul, MN. By good fortune, the Milwaukee Rail chose the Chicago-La Crosse route as its route west. After the Civil War cut off rail routes below the Ohio River, La Crosse became the most important terminal for freight and passengers heading west and north. Then came the lumber days.

Lumbering brought great prosperity to the town of La Crosse. The castles on Cass and the beautiful Victorian homes that abound in the residential section between downtown and Grandad bluff are a legacy of the lumber barons. Names like Hixon and Pettibone are reminders of the great wealth which was centered here.

What to See in La Crosse

LA-24
HIXON HOUSE (429 North Seventh Street). Historic 19th century home of wealthy lumberman from La Crosse's early commerical history. Unusual in that it is fully furnished, exactly as the Hixon's left it in the 1880's. Guided tours, small admission fee. Operated by the La Crosse County Historical Society.

A beautiful array of Victorian homes from this era is readily seen along Cass and Main Streets as you drive through La Crosse. A recommended free Heritage Tour of old La Crosse is available from the Swarthout Museum, the Hixon House or the Visitor and Convention Bureau office at Riverside Park.

Southside Oktoberfest Grounds are located at the west foot of La Crosse Street, just north of the Hixon House.

LA-25

PETTIBONE PARK (located on Barron Island opposite La Crosse central business district. Separated from city of La Crosse by the Main Channel of river. Access via Cass Street over the Main Channel Bridge). Park is named for the lumberman, A.W. Pettibone, who donated the land to the city in 1890. An RV resort is in the planning stages for Barron Island, at the south end of the park. Swimming beach with bathhouse • lagoon • playground • ice skating in winter on lagoon

La Crescent, MN, is located just beyond Pettibone Park. The *Apple Blossom Scenic Trail* which begins in La Crescent is clearly marked in the town and highly recommended. The short drive follows the Minnesota blufftops to Dakota, MN, with panoramic views of Lake Onalaska and the island-studded Mississippi.

LA-26

RIVERSIDE PARK (west foot of State Street in downtown La Crosse). Main 'showpiece' park on Mississippi River west of central business district. *Convention and Visitors Bureau Visitor Center* houses the *Riverside, USA* exhibit in which an animated Mark Twain tells tales of life along the Mississippi and the visitor can try his hand at piloting a riverboat. Call 784-8523 for information. The *La Crosse Queen* paddleboats are docked nearby.

Riverside Park is the site of the annual *Riverfest* held during the 4th of July weekend with live music, food tasting, and fireworks. Flower gardens • playground • picnicking • pleasant riverside walkway

The Central Business District is located between Second and Sixth Streets, with convenient access from Riverside Park.

LA-20 — LA-31

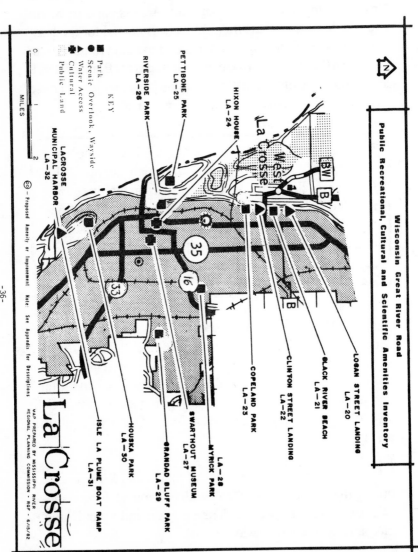

The *Pump House* is home to the regional arts association. Several galleries with changing displays and live performances. Located at west end of King Street.

G. Heileman Brewery Tours and Gift Shop is located south of the business district on Third Street between Market and Mississippi Streets. Tours of the brewery are offered several times a day.

LA-27
SWARTHOUT MUSEUM is located in La Crosse Public Library at 800 Main Street. First class county historical museum with periodically changing exhibits of river town history. No admission charge.

> **Continue east on Main Street from the library and north on 16th Street past UW-La Crosse to find Myrick Park.**

LA-28
MYRICK PARK (2000 block of La Crosse Street, between *STH 16* and La Crosse River marsh). Although this park is not located on the Great River Road or the Mississippi River, it is significant to the traveler because it overlooks the La Crosse River marshland and Mississippi River backwater area. Indian mounds are designated by a historical marker. Zoo • concession stand • kiddy rides • playgrounds • shelter houses • picnicking • wading pool • trails into marsh habitat

> **Continue east on La Crosse Street to Losey Blvd. South on Losey to Main Street and follow Main east up the bluff side to Grandad Bluff.**

LA-29

GRANDAD BLUFF (on Main Street, approximately two miles from the river). Scenic bluff 500+ feet above city with outstanding view of river valley and three states, as well as the City of La Crosse. Historical marker atop the bluff commemorates site of first Christian worship held in La Crosse by passengers from a river steamboat. From the lookout at the summit of the 150-acre park, it is possible to see 30 miles down river. Minnesota and Iowa are visible.

Hixon Forest is an adjacent 600-acre natural area of typical Mississippi River bluff forest and open habitat. According to Myer Katz *(Echos of our Past)* the forest was named to commemorate the family who purchased the bluff and donated it to the city after a gravel company served notice that it planned to harvest the lumber and reduce the bluff to a gravel pit. Picnicking • shelter house • hiking • cross-country ski trails

LA-30

HOUSKA PARK (at foot of Market Street. Accessible via Jackson St. and extensions across bridge to island.) Shelter house • picnicking • wading pool • playground

Looking for a place to eat? La Crosse has many fine restaurants. The *Freight House* is just east of Riverside park and adjacent to Christina's Winery. *Piggy's* and the *Radisson Hotel* both offer river views while dining. The *New Villa* and *Michaels* are both located at the south end of town along *STH 35).*

Losey Blvd., South Avenue and West Avenue (STH 35) all meet at the south end of La Crosse near Shelby Mall. The Great River Road continues south toward Stoddard, WI, from this point. The traveler interested in seeing what upland Wisconsin looks like might want to follow USH 14 toward Coon Valley and Norskedalen (see Vernon County) or STH 33 east past the K-Mart Mall.

Where Fishing is King

VERNON COUNTY

The Mississippi River between Goose Island County Park (just south of La Crosse) and DeSoto, WI, forms the western boundary of Vernon County. This 'west coast' of Vernon County provides an astonishing 8800 acres of Mississippi River access. Fishing on the river is outstanding year round, with fisherman parking, public and private boat launches, and marinas abundant along the Great River Road. River watching, birding and recreational boating are other major attractions. The county is two-thirds the size of the state of Rhode Island and boasts the prospect of 1600 miles of truly scenic and varied exploration.

An auto side trip to *Wildcat Mountain State Park* leads through the Amish community along *STH 33* between Cashton and Ontario. Excellent camping, horseback riding trails, and trout fishing are available at the park.

Canoe shuttle services are available in *Ontario* on *STH 33* for the *Kickapoo River*. The 100-mile-long Kickapoo River basin provides outstanding family canoeing. The generally placid river twists and turns through peaceful farmland and between dramatic rocky outcroppings.

Less than 20 miles from Wildcat Mountain is the *Elroy Sparta National Bike Trail*. The 32-mile gravel trail with overnight camping facilities follows an old railroad bed through several tiny villages and three unique railroad tunnels. This is fairly easy biking, especially if you start in Elroy as the trail has a slight downhill slope to Sparta. The trail will shortly be part of an extensive state trail which will wind around to La Crosse and then up the Great River Road through Perrot State Park to Alma.

Norskedalen, just north of *Coon Valley* on *USH 14* and *CTH P*, offers a unique look at the life of early Norwegian settlers in the area. Operated by the University of Wisconsin - La Crosse and local volunteers, it provides a cultural center, ethnic library, museum and authentic Norwegian log home and farm buildings, blacksmith shop, tools, and household furnishings. A different nature or cultural program is presented in the Center each Sunday afternoon. The Center is open weekdays and weekends throughout the summer, weekends during the winter, or by special arrangement. Small admission charge.

Two very small county parks provide beautiful picnic sites in the heart of Vernon County. *Sidie Hollow* is located out of Westby on *CTH XX*. The spring-fed pond at *Jersey Valley* on *CTH X* is clear enough to allow snorkling. Playgrounds and shelters are available at both parks.

Mount La Crosse, just south of the juncture of *USH 14* and *61* on *STH 35*, offers downhill and cross-country skiing throughout the winter.

The area also supports an unusual *turkey hunting* season. The county is at the heart of a successful effort by the Department of Natural Resources to reestablish the wild turkey.

SPECIAL EVENTS

MID-FEBRUARY	Westby, *Snowflake International 90 Meter Ski Jumping Tournament.* An F.I.S. USA sanctioned tournament at the Snowflake Ski Jump. Features teams from Norway, Finland, Canada, and USA.
Early MAY	Coon Valley, *Coon Creek Canoe Races* begin at Veterans Park.
3rd Weekend in MAY	Westby, *Syttende Mai.* Norwegian Constitution Day celebration. Commemorates independence from Danish rule in 1814. Ethnic food, music, dancing, crafts and quilt auction.
Early JUNE	*Viroqua Heritage Days.* Arts, crafts, tractor pull. Carnival and parade.
SEPTEMBER Labor Day Weekend	Stoddard, *Firemen's Picnic.* Water fights, chicken Q, softball, live music. Romance (southwest of Genoa), *Country Band Jamboree.* Food, beverages, and live music at the ball park.
Mid-SEPTEMBER	Viroqua, *Vernon County Fair.*

Geography

The drive from *Goose Island* to Victory, WI, is one of the most scenic in the Midwest. The ridges, steep valleys and towering sandstone bluffs are characteristic of this driftless corner of southwestern Wisconsin.

Goat Prairie is the name given to unique bald spots on south-facing bluff sides. The frequent thawing and freezing on these severe slopes makes their surfaces inhospitable to larger trees and brush. The steep slope also protects the plant life from grazing animals. Thus these unique areas are believed to provide the best example of the bluff's virgin prairie. Plants like the *Pasque Flower* which exist in few other spots in Wisconsin can still be found in these little plots.

Modern farm *soil and water conservation* techniques had their start in the county back in the 1930's. Farmers near Coon Valley realized that conventional up and down plowing on steep valleys resulted in damaging soil erosion. The resulting practice of *strip - cropping* appears as a unique undulating crop pattern from the air. It is apparent to the visitor as narrow alternating strips of corn, hay or other crops on the hillsides.

Strip-cropping (or contour farming) as seen from the air.

TOUR ROUTE: GOOSE ISLAND TO DESOTO

LA-33
GOOSE ISLAND PARK/CAMPGROUND *(CTH GI*, 4 miles south of La Crosse). A major, highly-recommended county park situated on several river islands . Pan-fishing is excellent along the causeway into the main park. There are over 400 campsites, some with electricity and a large, paved RV section. Swimming beach in campground area. Picnicking • birding • boating • shelters • playgrounds • convenience store • boat and canoe rentals

MOHAWK VALLEY RV SALES & SERVICE (1/4 mile south of Goose Island. Propane, some parts, and storage.

CLAMMING ON THE MISSISSIPPI

Commercial Clamming

Both Goose Island County Park and Blackhawk Park near Victory, WI, are likely spots to encounter your first *clamming boat,* a large, ungainly, flatbottomed craft with an overhead bar draped with lots of heavy line and hooks. Clamming, a traditional source of river income, has experienced a recent resurgence. Japan's cultured pearl industry, which has devastated the natural pearl industry, has increased demand for clam shells. The shells are ground into small shot size and inserted into oysters as starters for cultured pearls.

As clam beds to the south are deteriorating, more and more southern clammers are moving into the area. Recently, the first comprehensive legislation since the 1920's has been passed to control licensing, size and harvest of river clams.

The Pearl Button Industry

At the turn of the century, pearl button factories were found in several river towns, including Genoa. Round saws were used to cut *blanks* or circular pieces from a clam shell. The white pearl shells were often 1/2-inch or more thick. This blank was divided into several unfinished buttons which were ground on a traveling band that passed under grindstones. A depression was made in each disk and holes drilled for thread. The buttons were then smoothed, polished with pumice stone and water in revolving kegs, sorted and sewed on cards.

The "holey shells" and rough blanks can still be found in the soil around many river towns.

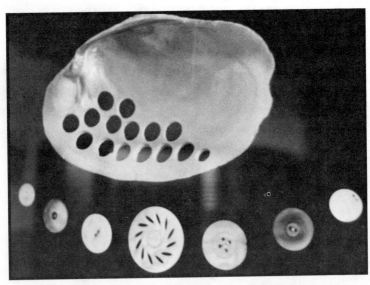

"Holey" clam shell with pearl button samples.

VE-1 through VE-5
FISHERMAN PARKING. VE-1, *Shady Maple,* is a popular fishing spot in all seasons. Ice shanty village pops up in winter to shelter undaunted fishermen. Stairs provide access to river, across railroad tracks. VE-2 also provides a stairway, the rest are trail only.

Note: Look both ways before crossing railroad tracks along the Great River Road. As many as 24 fast freight trains use these tracks each day.

STODDARD, WISCONSIN

Located seven miles south of La Crosse and situated on the sandy delta of Coon Creek, the village of Stoddard (population 760) was the center of a farming community that reached well out into the Mississippi before construction of the Genoa Lock and Dam. It is a popular fishing area. The town offers a boutique with locally-created crafts, an antique shop, and a convenient roadside *camping/dump station* at the Dreamland Motel. The local cafe and two supper clubs are both recommended and offer shuttle service from the Water's Edge, a picturesque privately owned marina/campground.

VE- 6
STODDARD RIVER PARK (west on Center Street, south on Pearl.) Safe (but unguarded) river beach • boat launch • fisherman parking • picnicking

There is an excellent view from the park of one of the widest spots in the upper Mississippi. The river here is almost five miles wide. The Minnesota bluffs with numerous ridges and steep valleys are usually clearly seen from the Wisconsin shore.

VE-1 through VE-4

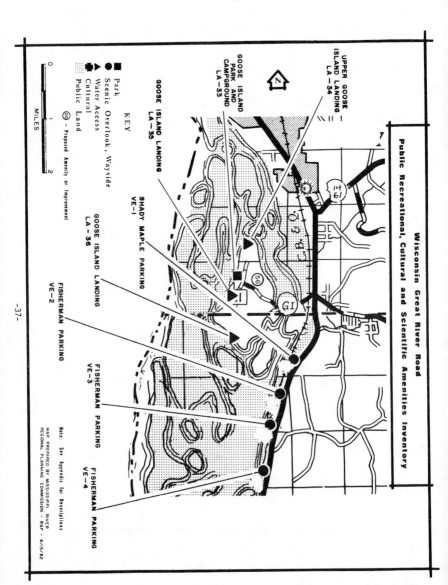

Much of the expanse of water between Stoddard and Genoa was created by the flooding of over 18,000 acres of prairie and farmland when the Genoa Lock & Dam was built in 1937. The many stump fields and north-south lying islands are remnants of field and woodland.

A Bit of Stoddard History

Located off the main Mississippi channel, Stoddard, unlike many neighboring villages, was never a river port. Instead it developed as a commercial center whose lifeblood was the Chicago, Burlington, and Northern Railroad. Ice, planed lumber, flour, and millions of pounds of fish were once shipped from the corner of Pearl and Center streets. The town was most likely named for Col. Thomas B. Stoddard, a La Crosse mayor who was instrumental in bringing the railroad through the village.

VE-7
STODDARD VILLAGE PARK (southeast edge of town on *STH 35*). There is often a tournament or special event happening in the park with food, beverages available. Excellent picnicking • playground • flush toilets • water • shelters • baseball diamond

VE-8
PULLOVER (west side, *STH 35*). Unofficial, unpaved pullover at delta - like area where Coon Creek empties into the Mississippi. Excellent birding area. Eagles, osprey, herons, egrets, and huge numbers of Canvasback ducks, Tundra swans and other waterfowl can be observed at close range during spring and fall migrations. The Stoddard and Lynxville areas are sanctuaries for migrating waterfowl. Closed to all hunting.

WAYSIDE (east side *STH 35* south of Stoddard). Rest area
overlooks the Mississippi. Picnic tables • water • pit toilets

> *Local history suggests that the first Norwegian set-*
> *tlers embarked from the river at this point; they walked along*
> *Coon Creek toward what is now the Coon Valley-Westby area,*
> *staking out farms as they passed. This is the Township of*
> *Bergen.*

VE-9
OLD SETTLERS OVERLOOK (east side *STH 35).* Road
winds up the side of 500 foot bluff. Abandoned rock quarry
is now a scenic overlook. Excellent photo spot in all seasons.
Hiking trails give access to additional river views and natural
wooded/prairie areas. Three states are visible: Minnesota,
Iowa and Wisconsin. Picnic tables • grills • water • shelter •
toilets

BECK'S FISHERY (east side *STH 35).* The various fish
markets along this southern portion of the Great River Road
make interesting stops. Each commercial fisherman has his
own niche in the market. One might sell fresh fish locally,
another ships to metropolitan areas, while another does spe-
ciality processing. The fisherman and his family are usually
on the premises, in the process of cleaning fish or preparing
lines.

VE-10
GENOA VILLAGE PARK (east side of *STH 35).* Not directly
on the river. Picnicking • shelter • toilets • tennis courts •
baseball • playground equipment

ENGH'S FISH MARKET *(east of STH 35).* {} **Overnight
camping for $3.** Camping with electricity is $5.00. Showers
• toilets

By mid-morning, most of the day's catch has been unloaded and visitors are usually welcome to have a look. Expect huge tubs of catfish, bullhead, sheepshead, and carp of all sizes. There is usually a collection of nasty big snapping turtles hibernating in the walk-in refrigerator. The fish markets are also the place to see some of the river's oddities —a 57 lb. buffalo fish, a paddlefish, or a giant catfish.

GENOA, WISCONSIN

A picturesque fishing village with a "Little Italy" flavor, Genoa offers motels, camping, cafe, fishing supplies and gift shop. Follow *Old Hwy 35* for a drive through town. Original settlers had varied ethnic backgrounds but the Italian seem to have prevailed. Names like Zabolio, Trussoni, Pedretti, Nickelatti, and Furlano are commonplace. The Zabolio store on Main Street was run by the same family for 100 years before being sold in 1980.

The Catholic Church, *St. Charles Borromeo,* is and always has been the only church in town. It is perched, like many of the homes, well above the main street, with its cemetery continuing up the bluff side in a most precarious manner. There is a scenic outlook from the very top of the old cemetery from the steps of a monument built in memory of WWI vets. RVers who would like to visit this cemetery should park at the church and walk up as the road is narrow and winding.

Genoa and many other river town cemeteries offer scenic outlooks, as they were built well up the bluffs to avoid contamination of the village water source.

A Bit of Genoa History

The earliest settlers came to the Genoa area from Galena, IL, dissatisfied with mining and lumbering conditions to the south. Many of the settlers who followed came directly from from the northern, alpine regions of Italy and Switzerland. The county and the town were originally called Bad Ax (spelled without an 'e'). The village name was changed in 1868 to honor the home town of Christopher Columbus. By that time, Genoa had become a busy steamboat landing and many immigrants found ready employment. The local men were later employed on section gangs building and maintaining track for the Chicago, Burlington and Northern Railroad.

VE-11
GENOA BOAT LANDING, MARINA (west side of *STH 35*).

VE-12
LOCK & DAM #8 (south side of Genoa). *Visitors welcomed* to view lock & dam operations from viewer platform. Information on locking process and responsibilities of Army Corps of Engineers to maintain 9 ft. deep shipping channel. Parking
• toilets • water

VE-13
WAYSIDE/FISHERMAN PARKING (east side of *STH 35*). Scenic overlook. Historical marker describing navigational lock & dam system. Stairs across railroad track to riverside fishing and picnicking area.

Access to commercial fishing barge via ferry service is available from fishing area. There are commercial fishing barges located below each of the dams along the river. Excellent opportunity for the traveler to experience some of the best fishing in the mid-west for about $6. *The water below the dam will not freeze during the winter, making this a likely spot to see wintering eagles fishing for dead or injured fish.*

VE-14
DAIRYLAND POWER PLANT (west of *STH 35*). Site of one of the first nuclear power plants in the USA. Currently operating only the coal burning plant.

FISHERMAN PARKING/BOAT LAUNCH. Turn sharp left before entering Dairyland Power Plant and follow un-paved road to boat landing.

"Butch" and Gina Engh pose with rare 45 pound catfish.

INSIGHT

"BUTCH" ENGH
COMMERCIAL FISHERMAN

There have definitely been dramatic changes on the river in the 30 years that I've lived and fished here. The shorelines and islands are being eroded and the wash or sediment is filling in many of the river's deeper holes and ravines. The Army Corps of Engineers is maintaining a 9 foot deep channel for shipping, but the river bottom is flattening out and is relatively higher than it has been in the past.

This makes fishing a little more difficult as the fish seem to be constantly on the move —fish need these deeper holes for shelter in both winter and summer. As the river is flattening out, these holes are disappearing and the fish are changing their patterns.

Also, as the river bottom gets higher, we're seeing more flooding, more swamp, as there are no longer deep areas to contain flood water. When you look out there, it seems like a lot of water. Much of it, though, is too shallow to take a boat into.

Something that affects our business is the occasional warning not to eat large river fish. People who hear that aren't going to rush down to the local grocery to buy fresh fish — and there goes our market for the week. What people don't always realize is that fish large enough to be included in the warning are a size that is very seldom caught. The warnings are for those who eat huge quantities of large fish, not the 3 to 5 pounders that are typically sold.

On a typical day, I'll go out early morning to bring in the catch from the set lines. We'll have breakfast, then set to work cleaning and processing the catch. The lines have to be cleaned, untangled and rebaited which is called 'running a line.'

Mid-day I might go out again with the gill nets, these monofilament nets that you see drying occasionally along river banks. I'll come back and then go out again to lay out the set lines, baited with minnows, leeches, grasshoppers or whatever the catfish are biting on at the time. It's usually 9 p.m. before we have supper around here.

Yes, we eat fish. Usually three or four times a week — sometimes three times a day.

VE-15
FISHERMAN PARKING (south of Genoa, 1 mile north of Fish Hatchery). Note islands, sloughs, backwater as opposed to the wide pool north of the dam.

FROH'S CABINS (east side *STH 35*). Fisherman cabins sleep five. Kitchen, dishes, linen. Clean. Approximately $27/ night. $150/week. *Such inexpensive fisherman lodging, often with kitchenette and dishes, but no TV, is abundant along the river.*

VE-16
NATIONAL FISH HATCHERY (at mouth of Bad Ax River, just before bridge). Native fish species are raised for stocking rivers in the Upper Midwest. Informal viewing of rearing ponds. Formal tours by arrangement. Toilets • water

VE-5 — VE-14

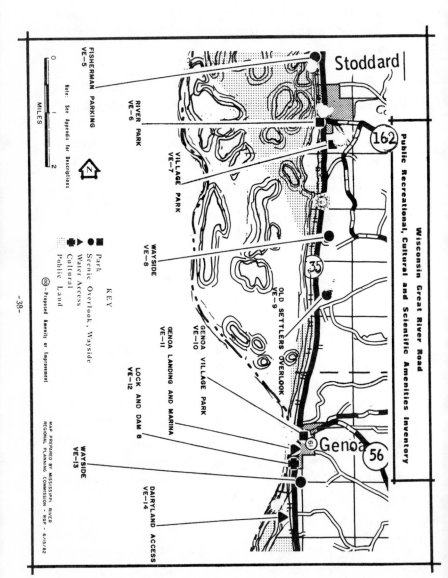

VE-17

BAD AX BOAT LANDING (just south of National Fish Hatchery, after the bridge over the Bad Ax River). Follow the gravel road west to the well developed boat landing. Good shore fishing is possible. Parking • toilets • picnicking

According to an account written by George Gale in 1860, the river was named Bad Ax because the Indians found the local limestone too soft to make a good ax. This theory rings true as much of the success of an Indian tribe depended on the quality of stone readily available for tool-making. An even older theory suggests that the name may have come from the Indian pronunciation of the French word for 'boats' which was 'batteaux.'

The county name was changed from Bad Ax to Vernon in 1861 after it had long been plagued by the pun, "Bad Acts," relating the name to the character of the rivermen.

VICTORY, WISCONSIN

Victory was once the principal steamboat landing between La Crosse and Galena, IL. A major stockyard was located along the tracks for loading stock onto the trains to Chicago and Minnesota farmers would swim their stock from island to island across the river to bring them to the yards.

The excursion steamer, *J.S.*, which traveled the river between Lansing and La Crosse burned to the water just off the docks of Victory. Most excursion boats included a jail in the hold for rowdy passengers. It was thought that such a drunken passenger started this fire. Conflicting reports indicate that no one was hurt, though the rowdy passenger was never heard of again.

While Victory now has mainly summer and retirement homes, several of the old hotels are still standing.

The Battle of Bad Ax

The most significant bit of local history is the *Black Hawk War of 1832*, of which the locally fought Battle of Bad Ax was the decisive battle. Troops from Fort Crawford at Prairie du Chien had succeeded in driving Black Hawk and his Fox/Sac followers from the Wisconsin Dells area to the edge of the Mississippi. Aided by additional volunteers from Galena, IL, and the stockade at Pepin and by cannon aboard the steamer *Warrior,* the starving band of Indians was massacred near the present town of Victory as they attempted to escape with their women and children across the maze of islands to the Minnesota shore.

Black Hawk escaped this massacre, but was captured shortly after by his bitter enemies the Sioux, who delivered him to the American Army. As a prisoner of the American Army, he was displayed throughout the 'civilized' world.

Local names, such as *Battle Hollow, Battle Island, Red Mound, Victory,* and *Retreat* are reminiscent of this battle. Zachary Taylor, Abraham Lincoln, Jefferson Davis and Henry Dodge were among many well-known officers at the time of the Indian Wars. All of them pointed to their part in this and other Indian battles during campaigns for public office.

Settlers followed rapidly after the Black Hawk War, first from Illinois, then in droves from Scandinavia, Italy, Germany, and Switzerland. Even the Irish and the English were represented along the river basin.

Black Hawk and his war have been commemorated up and down the Mississippi River Valley. Each town has its Black Hawk Park, hotel, saloon or cafe. Museums located in Galena and Rock Island, IL, as well as La Crosse and Red Mound, WI, have exhibits dating from the Black Hawk War. The local history museum at Red Mound, near Victory, is right off *STH 35* on *CTH UU*.

VE-18

VICTORY LANDING (at community of Victory). A local boat launch with difficult maneuvering. Unguarded railroad crossing.

VE-19

BLACKHAWK COUNTY PARK (1 mile south of Victory on west side of *STH 35*). This is a major river park operated by the Army Corps of Engineers. Campsites along backwater are abundant with excellent shore fishing. $7/night. 50% discount for Senior Citizens at **all** Corps of Engineers campgrounds. 2 paved boat launches • picnic tables • shelters • small store • boat rental

VE-20

BAD AX WAYSIDE (east side of Great River Road, 1 mile north of Town of DeSoto). Historical marker commemorating the Battle of Bad Ax.

Look to the northeast to see an excellent example of a bluff-side "goat prairie." When the French fur traders, Indians and buffalo were roving throughout this area, Wisconsin was largely prairie or oak savanna rather than the woodlands which now clothe the ridges and valleys; thus names like "Prairie La Crosse," "Prairie Du Chien," "Sauk (or Sac) Prairie."

VE-15 — CR-1

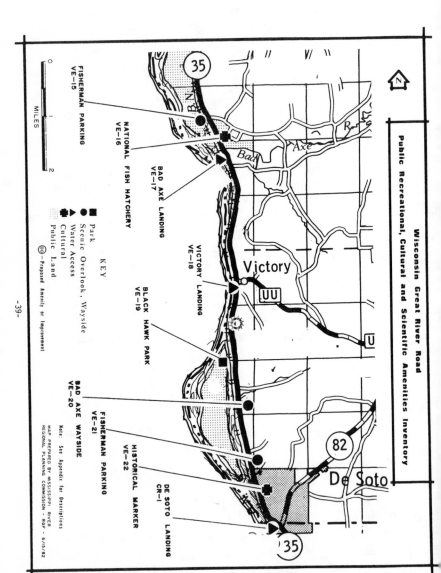

VE-21
FISHERMAN PARKING (north of DeSoto village limits).
15 parking places • scenic overlook.

VE-22
HISTORICAL MARKER (just north of DeSoto, on west
side). Historical marker commemorating Winnebago Chief,
Winnisheik. Small turn-off area.

DESOTO, WISCONSIN

Named for Spanish explorer, Fernando DeSoto,
who was the first white man to see the Mississippi River.
After he died in 1542, DeSoto was buried in the Mississippi.

DeSoto was originally the site of a Winnebago village called *Winnesheik*. According to an old newspaper story,
travelers could overnight in the area at a French fur trader's
cabin and pass away the hours playing euchre for hickory nuts.

Most villages were also strategically located near
river valleys which provided a passable route inland. Eventually DeSoto became an important port city along the Mississippi. The Captain's Cafe, along *STH 35*, is an excellent spot
for homemade pies and local chatter. The village park, with
toilets and picnicking area is located to the immediate right of
the Captain's Cafe.

CR-1
DESOTO LANDING (south edge of village limits). Boat
landing, parking area.

CR-2
WINNESHEIK SLOUGH (*STH 82*, west of *STH 35* and Burlington Northern Railroad). Boat launch.

BOARDMAN'S FISH MARKET (just south of village of DeSoto before the Lansing Bridge) is another little commercial fishery. Specialty fish processing includes fish jerky, and bologna as well as the usual fresh and smoked fishes. Will ship fresh on ice throughout the USA. *Camping* with electricity, some sewered sites. Few large level sites.

THE LANSING BRIDGE (*STH 82*). Crosses river bottoms and main channel to Lansing, IA.

The Great River Road splits off here and the traveler may choose to continue on Wisconsin STH 35 or to cross the river on STH 82, to Lansing, IA. Iowa's Great River Road passes the Effigy Mounds National Monument, dallies in historic McGregor and then crosses back into Wisconsin on the bridge to Prairie du Chien. See Chapter 8.

Wisconsin's Great River Road continues to the south, beyond the Lansing Bridge to Prairie du Chien, clinging to the edge of the bluffs, with the railroad and the river well below. A strikingly scenic portion of the route. See Chapter 9.

Commercial fisherman with morning's haul.

Outlook from the Genoa cemetery.

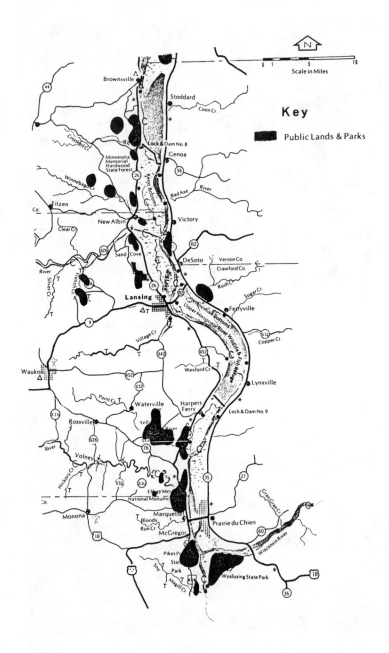

N

Scale in Miles

Brownsville

Stoddard

Coon Cr.

Key

Public Lands & Parks

Re

Lock & Dam No. 8

Genoa

Minnesota
Memorial
Hardwood
State Forest

56

Winnebago Cr.

Bad Axe   River

Fitzen

Co.

New Albin

Victory

Clear Cr.

82

Sand Cove

DeSoto

Vernon Co.

Crawford Co.

River

Silver Cr.

Rush Cr.

Sugar Cr.

Lansing

Ferryville

9

Upper Mississippi River Wildlife & Fish Refuge

174

Village Cr.

Copper Cr.

142

452

Waukon

Wexford Cr

452

232

Lynxville

Paint Cr.

Waterville

Harpers
Ferry

Lock & Dam No. 9

X19

Rossville

Yell

River

A26

76

Volney

27

Hickory Cr.

232

35

Elkhart Mou...
National Monum...

Co.

Monona

Cran Crane Cr.

Bloody

Marquette

Prairie du Chien

60

Run Cr.

McGregor

18

Wisconsin River

Pikes P

State

Park

Spy

Wyalusing State Park

18

Magill Cr.

35

Iowa's Surprising Northeast Corner

ALLAMAKEE AND CLAYTON COUNTIES

STH 82, the causeway from south of DeSoto, WI, to Lansing, IA, is an excursion through three miles of wilderness river bottoms. Numerous sloughs, islands, and backwater marshes are inhabited only by wildlife, waterfowl, fishes, and fishermen.

Iowa's Great River Road proceeds south from Lansing on *X52* for a beautiful drive through Harpers Ferry, Marquette and McGregor. This short route will take the traveler through a scenic portion of the state that is often referred to as *Iowa's Little Switzerland.* Indian Mounds seem to be clustered in the area of Harpers Ferry and are easily seen in that small town or at the *Effigy Mounds National Monument.* For campers, canoers and trout fishermen, the *Yellow River Forest State Recreation Area* and *Pike's Peak State Park* offers excellent camping, hiking, fishing, and scenic overlooks.

LANSING, IOWA

This picturesque village rests demurely in a small valley between the bluffs. The traveler crossing the iron lacework of the Blackhawk Bridge is greeted by the beautiful limestone house of Lansing's founder tucked mid-way up the *Mt. Hosmer* bluff-side. Named after Lansing, MI, the area has a rich heritage encompassing the wonders of the Indian

Mound Builders, Indian wars, steamboat trade, commercial fishing, and clamming.

Architecturally, Lansing is unique because there are so many limestone buildings still standing from the mid-1800's. Both the *Old Stone School (1848)* and the *Grain Elevator* (1868) on Front Street have been restored and are on the National Register of Historic Places. The limestone school is open to the public and can be found by turning right on John Street at the ball diamond. The former grain elevator now houses *The Sport and Gift Shop* on Front Street.

Local historians Bill and Derva Burke operate the Sport Shop. The wood bins, elevators, and mechanisms of the grain elevator are all intact. It is easy to envision paddleboats pulling up along the riverside to be filled with grain. The train still runs right past the front of the building, so park well forward.

The shop maintains a wildlife art gallery, an excellent collection of books on the river-lore of the upper Mississippi, and locally produced crafts. On weekends, the small *Sand Cove Queen* excursion boat leaves from the docks behind the building. A daily excursion to Prairie du Chien is in the planning stage.

The baseball diamond and playground now occupy the area which once housed numerous sawmills. The town was also a major shipping point for grain from Iowa and Wisconsin.

Not to be missed is the view from 400-foot-high *Mt. Hosmer.* This extensive city park is at the top of the bluff at the north end of town and contains five scenic overlooks from which three states (MN, WI, IA) and the great expanse of the

Mississippi and its backwaters are visible. The first of the hairpin turns going up the hill is VERY sharp, so take care, if driving a big rig.   Picnicking • toilets • water • shelter

There are several cafes and restaurants in town, including *Clancy's* for fine (but casual) dining and the *Waterfront Tavern* (short-order, with great river watching from the tables). Two Bed and Breakfast Inns operate in Lansing: *Fitzgerald's Inn,* a country home dating from 1863, and the *Lansing House,* a riverfront home beside the Blackhawk Bridge.

A full service marina is found north of town, while *S&S Houseboat Rentals* is located south of town. Both will offer overnight boat docking if space is available. Courtesy docks right off Main Street for river traffic. Easy walk to dining from these, or shuttle services from *S&S.*

The *Fish Farm Mounds State Preserve* is a cluster of 30 prehistoric Indian mounds located eight miles north of Lansing on *STH 26.* Clusters of Indian mounds are visible in several spots along the Iowa shore. The animal-shaped (effigy) mounds and cave drawings belong to Indian cultures dating back several thousand years.

The *Fish Market* (Lansing Fisheries) on the south end of Front Street is the largest between here and St. Louis. Each day, four or five workers will clean as much as 1500 pounds of fish fillets to ship with scales on to markets in Chicago and New York. The fish is shipped fresh in refrigerated trucks. The visitor may also see a soft-shelled or snapping turtle being butchered. The meat sells locally for $2.50 a pound and is tasty in turtle soup or when fried or grilled like chicken.

The new *City Boat Launch is* on Village Creek. Turn right, south of town, at the first fork in the road and then a quick left onto a gravel road with large area for fisherman parking. Concrete ramps • no other amenities

> **Follow X52 south out of Lansing**
> **13 miles to Harpers Ferry, IA**

Fisherman Parking and Access is provided by the Iowa State DNR (Department of Natural Resources) at the entrance to the Interstate Power plant just south of Lansing.

A second *DNR Boat Launch and Parking Area* is located directly on the Mississippi, but is a good two miles off X52 through farmland. This pleasant little side trip follows a dry creek bed down from the highland to the riverbottom through a deep, picturesque hollow, complete with a broad meadow and old log barn. In season, the strip cropping of corn and alfalfa is easily seen on hillsides. The boat launch area is well maintained and quiet. There are no picnic tables or water.

Just beyond the turn off for the boat launch, X52 begins its descent to the river's edge. The congregation of the *Wexford Church* has provided a roadside rest area with a beautiful rock/flower garden. The guest register includes visitors from throughout the USA and the world.

The historic limestone church and cemetery were begun in 1848 by an Irish congregation with ties to the county of Wexford in Ireland. This is one of the few cemeteries along the route where century-old tombstones are engraved in English rather than one of the European languages.

HARPERS FERRY, I OWA

The village of Harpers Ferry is planted on a sandy plateau about one mile wide along the edge of the river. A friendly, quiet village mid-week, it becomes a rousing little fishing town on the weekends. Its winter population of 250 swells to nearly 4000 during the summer as snowbirds return and vacationers fill summer cabins up and down the river.

The tiny village is located across the river from Lynxville, WI, and ten miles north of Prairie du Chien. Settler David Harper provided farmers and businessmen with ferry service to the main channel and market place at Lynxville.

The town is built upon a concentrated area of *Indian Burial Mounds. Conical, linear,* and *effigy mounds* are apparent both in town and beyond either end. The City Park has a marker explaining the mounds in greater detail. As you drive along the river road in town, the mounds are easily visible in the park.

The *End of the Line Sport Shop and Marina* in the village provides cabin, boat and motor rental. The road just above The End of the Line leads to a parking spot for visitors to the historic *Sandy Point Cemetery*. The Pines Cafe and Motel has motel rooms, as well as trailer and cabin rental.

The Sandy Point Cemetery was begun in 1859. The pathway to the cemetery is interesting in its own right, as it follows the edge of a plateau about 40 ft. above the river. Clearly visible are several conical mounds. The cemetery was closed to further burials in the 1920's after the "laid out" body of a man was found floating in the river. It was discovered that the cemetery was being eroded, releasing caskets and bodies into the river.

A Brief History of Lansing and Harpers Ferry History

Harpers Ferry and Lansing, IA, are in the middle of a region that was once favored Indian hunting grounds — for the Sioux to the north, and the Sac and Fox to the south. Because of frequent hostilities between the tribes, the U.S. government finally assigned the more peaceable Winnebagoes to occupy the area as a "buffer" between their aggressive neighbors. Thus it was the Winnebagoes who occupied the Harpers Ferry townsite prior to the arrival of the white man. An archaeological survey in 1892 revealed 895 Indian mounds in the "Harpers Ferry Great Group."

The area around Harpers Ferry was opened for settlement in 1848 after Indian title to the land had been extinguished. To the south, McGregor, Prairie du Chien, and Galena were already thriving cities on the western frontier. Immigrants and entrepreneurs were anxious to develop more territory. As Indian hostility to the west still presented grave danger to the traveler, development up-river blossomed.

A lime kiln, hotels, and ferry service to the eastern side of the river were the earliest industries in the area. Harpers Ferry would become an important steamboat landing although it was off the main channel of the Mississippi. Trapping, clamming, and commercial fishing among the maze of sloughs, backwaters, and wooded islands between the bluffs continue to be an important part of the economy.

Increasing leisure time since the World Wars has made

it possible for Harpers Ferry to survive its decline as a port city and prosper as a fishing resort. As more leisure time became available, people started thinking of going down to the river for the weekend. Today, summertime residents swell the many riverside resorts and trailer courts.

While visiting in Harpers Ferry, I had the pleasure of meeting local historian, Lil Taylor, who researches and speaks about the history of life on the river. Lil has provided the information for the 'History of Lansing/Harpers Ferry above and on the naming of local sloughs which follows. pm

WHAT'S THE NAME OF THAT SLOUGH??!

The backwaters of the Mississippi behind Harpers Ferry are a veritable maze of sloughs, islands, marshes—true Mississippi Bayoux. The unique names of sloughs up and down the river often commemorate some long-forgotten adventure or discovery by the men who made their living on the river.

BARGE HALL LAKE (Barge Haul Lake). Years ago when barges were employed by island farmers to take their grain, lumber and stock to market, a barge sank in this lake. Later a commercial fisherman, hoping to make a good fish haul here, caught and tore his nets on the sunken barge; so it became known as the Lake of the Barge Haul.

GUN LAKE. This seems to have been the name of this lake for as long as anyone can remember. Several fishermen recall having been told that a couple of boats in a duck hunting party overturned here, and all the guns were lost in the lake.

HOG SLOUGH. So called because a fearsome wild hog believed to have escaped from a local farm lived on the island. It was known to have survived two winters in the brush. It was never captured and presumably drowned in high water.

PIGEON SLOUGH. In early spring, the land adjacent to this slough was covered with a thick white blanket of the eggs of Passenger Pigeons. The fishermen reported seeing trees here virtually alive with pigeons. Today the Passenger Pigeon, once referred to as a 'living wind', is extinct.

SLEEPING POND. This large quiet body of water is a natural resting spot for wild geese during their flight south. Before there was a daily bag limit on water fowl, hunters took thousands of ducks here during the fall. It was not uncommon for a hunter to bag hundreds of waterfowl in a day. Every year, many southbound flocks still choose this pond as a place to rest—or sleep, as the river men term it.

WHITE RAT ISLAND. One year, trappers caught an albino muskrat here and every year for a number of years they trapped at least one more mutated muskrat from this lake. Each year there was a little less white until finally the muskrats showed no further white markings.

JUG HANDLE SLOUGH. Backwater area where fishermen regularly found dozens of jugs, all tied together by the handles. Suspected to be floating away from a liquor still hidden on one of the islands.

> **Tour Route: Harpers Ferry to McGregor, IA**
> *on STH 364*

ANDY'S MOUNTAIN CAMPGROUND south of Harpers Ferry on *STH 364* .   Full hook-ups • hiking

The Yellow River Forest State Recreation Area is north on *STH 364*. Follow 364 up the bluff and past St. Joseph's cemetery, then left on the gravel road at the sign. The road follows a ridge-top, with the hill sloping away sharply from either side. Several large camping areas, canoeing and trout fishing are available in the recreation area. An Iowa user's permit is required.

The Iowa DNR maintains several riverside public use areas between Harpers Ferry and McGregor. The *Harpers Slough Public Use* area is an extended river's edge park with benches and shorefishing. *Nobles Island Public Use* area is a well maintained DNR boat landing and picnic area. Picnic tables • toilets • parking • artesian well

ARTESIAN WELLS

There is an artesian well flowing in the picnic area at the *Nobles Island Public Use Area*. Artesians are quite common throughout the coulee region and are often visible from the Great River Road, spewing out as much as 55 gallons per minute and more. Before the 1920's, the artesians provided drinking water for man and livestock and water to fight fires or power early backyard electrical plants.

The Iowa Department of Natural Resources has provided the following explanation of why an artesian is free flowing.

Artesian wells are created by drilling through impermeable rock layers into water-saturated sand aquifers. The water in these aquifers must be of sufficient pressure to rise above the immediate ground elevation. The water source and the pressure for this artesian well is illustrated below.

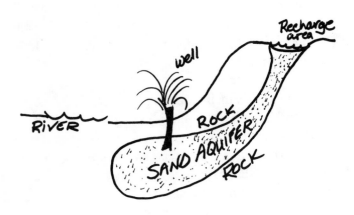

The water pressure in a free-flowing artesian is generated by a 'recharge' source that is above the point where the artesian well enters the aquifer. As the rainfall and run-off is absorbed in the recharge area the surface water seeps into the sand and flows downward into this valley. There are impermeable rock layers on both sides of this aquifer which prevents the water from escaping.

Thus by drilling a well which is below the recharge area, pressure in the sand aquifer is released and a flowing artesian well is obtained.

JUNCTION WITH *STH 76* AND *364*.
Effigy Mounds National Monument 3 Miles
Marquette, IA 7 Miles

Iowa STH 76 gradually winds its way inland and to the top of a ridge, where the hillsides fall away steeply from both sides of the road. There are sweeping views in all directions of fields and pastures.

EFFIGY MOUNDS NATIONAL MONUMENT. *Visitor Center,* tours, and slide show explaining the Indian Mound Culture. Open Memorial Day to Labor Day. Panoramic views of the Mississippi River and neighboring bluffs from the hiking trail which, after a fairly steep incline, meanders among Bear, Bird, and Turtle effigies dating back to 500 B.C. The progression from conical to linear and effigy mounds is well illustrated by trail markers. The monument contains 1,475 acres of wooded bluffs with a collection of 196 prehistoric Indian mounds.

The National Park ranger will point out that the building of mounds held great significance for the prehistoric Indians. The mounds have remained intact for thousands of years because they are capped with clay which was hauled from the river's edge to the top of the bluff. Some may have been burial mounds, some were not. The Mississippi River Valley was once covered with mounds, the legacy of a culture that persisted for over 1000 years in the past. Most have been destroyed by the farmer's plow or amateur archaeologists during the past 100 years.

The *Upper Mississippi River National Wildlife and Fish Refuge Visitor Center* located along the river between Marquette and McGregor is the headquarters for the McGregor District Office of the nation's longest, oldest and most popular wildlife refuge. The Upper Mississippi Refuge represented the first major conservation victory of the Izaak Walton League back in 1924. The group succeeded in convincing Congress to allocate funds for the purchase of land from private parties in order to establish the refuge. This was the first time Congress participated in the purchase of private land and permanently forestalled pressure from agricultural interests to have the Mississippi diked just south of DeSoto, WI.

Camping, boating, swimming, hunting, fishing and trapping are all allowed in the refuge, except in marked areas which have been set aside as sanctuaries.

The refuge protects much of the *Mississippi River Flyway* which is the natural north-south migration route for hundreds of different species of birds and waterfowl through the area.

The Mississippi River Flyway is a major north-south migration route.

MC GREGOR, IOWA

McGregor touts itself as a tiny Galena — "They're bigger and more sophisticated, but we've got the Mississippi River!" And how right they are. While Galena is truly an architectural treasure, the restored Main Street of McGregor, nestled deep into a pocket surrounded by bluffs, is a delightful jewel.

Upon arrival in McGregor, first stop will likely be Triangle Park. *The Visitor Information Booth* is located in this tiny downtown park across from the McGregor winery. Across the street is the *Little Switzerland Inn* with delicious French pastries.

The Shoquogon Trading Company, headquartered at the log cabin next to the Little Switzerland Bakery, offers a unique opportunity to experience a canoe voyage *'a la voyageur.'* The 26-foot replica trading canoe has a two-man crew in period costume and can carry up to 10 passengers. The 3-hour voyage includes a sandbar stop, wine and French cheese. For further information call (319) 753-1667.

The lengthy Main Street offers many antique and specialty shops. The *Alexander Hotel and Cafe* and the *RiverTown Inn* offer accomodations. It is probably best to make reservations to prevent disappointment.

If you follow McGregor's main street right out of town, Pike's Peak is located about three miles to the south on *STH 340.* Panoramic views of the confluence of the Wisconsin river and the Mississippi are visible from parking areas at Pike's Peak.

Spook Cave is off to the northwest about five miles and offers a boat tour almost two miles long on an underground river. Here is a convenient opportunity to touch a cephalopod fossil and hear a few (cheerfully admitted) corny jokes. Scenic *camping* with full hook-ups.

Both stops are recommended. There is a poetic contrast between the soaring bluff-top views at Pike's Peak and the underground boat tour at Spook Cave.

Overlook at Pike's Peak State Park

A Brief History of Clayton County

A history of the twin villages of McGregor and Marquette (originally named North McGregor) introduces Spain, a fourth nation to hold dominion over portions of the Upper Mississippi. The claim of Basil Giard in the 1780's was one of three Spanish claims granted in the current state of Iowa.

McGregor was once part of Spain's Louisiana Territory, which was ceded to the Americans in the Louisiana Purchase. The Sioux chief, Wapasha, is credited with preventing any further northern movement by the Spanish along the Mississippi.

Permanent settlement of the area did not begin until 1837 when a young Scot by the name of Alexander McGregor purchased the portion of the Giard claim located in a ravine across from the bustling trading center known as Prairie du Chien.

By 1870, 5000 people lived in McGregor, providing goods and services for the westward movement. August Ringling and his family moved into the area in 1860. His son, Al, offered his first 'pin and penny' circus in McGregor before leaving at age 21 to promote the "Greatest Show on Earth."

Sixty-eight trains a day brought goods and passengers into the developing railway complex at North McGregor. Over 60 industries, from saddleries to breweries provided employment and supplies for immigrants pouring into the new world. As farmers established themselves inland, McGregor became the most important port for sending agricultural products east to market.

McGregor's small ferry which was poled along by crew and passengers soon gave way to a larger vessel powered by several horses or mules treading a circular walkway in the center of the ferry. In 1858, the first railroad cars were ferried across the river from Prairie du Chien. From 1874 to 1961, the railroad crossed the Mississippi on a pontoon bridge, the first and largest of its kind in the world.

Increasing population along the western bank of the Mississippi, the development of other ports, and the decline of the railroad resulting from improved road systems all lead to the gradual decline of the two McGregors. The architectural treasure left to present day McGregor is a legacy of the area's boom period when nearly 6000 people lived in the four ravines leading to the bluff tops.

Today, the scenic beauty of the area, the restored old buildings and the excellent fishing again draw tens of thousands of visitors through the area. The highway now skirts bluffs which long prevented any land travel to the north or south, but for North McGregor and McGregor, IA, it was the routes east and west that made all the difference.

> *The night I stayed in McGregor, I had to choose between a room with a panoramic view, a balcony room overhanging the Grand River itself, or a B&B in a restored 1870's building. Nice choice! But for me, the big draw is the river, and I was rewarded by a mild, bugless evening spent watching the last of the day's barges surge upriver.*
>
> *Awoke to the pinkish cast of early sunrise washing over the river-edge. From my window I see the boat docks, 3 well-maintained buildings with frontier fronts, a log cabin, and a cobblestone street.*
>
> *The wooded islands of the Mississippi surround this little haven to the east; the Great River Road curves out of sight behind grand bluffs to the north; and, to the west, the ravine sweeps upward to complete a great buffer around the entire town.*
>
> *While I know perfectly well that Prairie du Chien lies three miles to the east, and that La Crosse is 70 miles up-river, I simply don't believe it. I feel enveloped in greenery, encased in a distant time.*
>
> *pm*

McGregor, IA, against a backdrop of bluffs.

McGregor's restored Main Street — photo by June Kuefler

CR-1 — CR-5

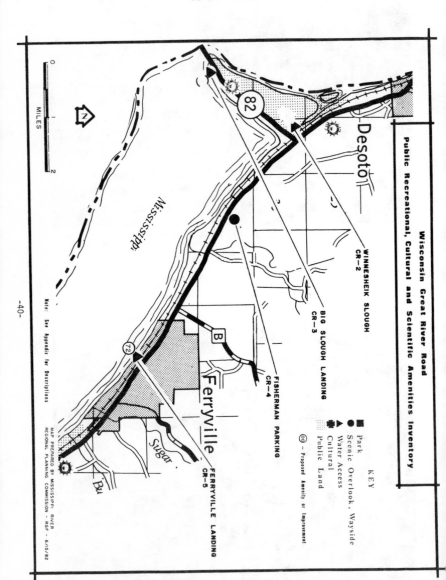

Rendezvous!

PRAIRIE DU CHIEN
AND
CRAWFORD COUNTY

The traveler who has opted to follow the river road between Ferryville and Prairie du Chien will be well rewarded as a good portion of the route is etched into bluffsides which plunge directly into the river. Often, there seems to be barely enough room for both *STH 35* and the railroad to cling to the cascading river bluffs.

Crawford County has a total of 60 miles of river borders, including the historic *Wisconsin River* along its southern edge. A third major river, the *Kickapoo,* continues its meanderings from Vernon County to finally join the Wisconsin in the village of Wauzeka on *STH 60.* Although this most crooked river provides 100 miles of scenic canoeing, its total length is only about 33 linear miles. Its Indian name, *Kwigapawa,* means "it moves about here and there."

There are several scenic drives accessible from the Great River Road. *STH 27* from Prairie du Chien north through Eastman to *Gays Mills* is a skyline drive that gradually drops into the Kickapoo River Valley where, in season, thousands of blooming apple trees decorate the hill-sides.

STH 131 north of Wauzeka follows the Kickapoo River to the Vernon County border and the solar village of *Soldier's Grove*. The town has been rebuilt above the flood plain of the Kickapoo and has incorporated solar energy construction into all the new commercial buildings. Gays Mills and Soldiers Grove are also easily visited by following *STH 171* from the Great River Road just south of Ferryville.

The Great River itself takes on the maze-like appearance of pre-lock and dam days, dissected into channels and sloughs, islands and backwaters, and occasional broad stretches of grassy prairie.

The contrast between the broad pool just north of the dam and the bayoux below the dam are typical of the 'pool' structure imposed upon the river by the lock and dam system. Typically, there will be the narrow main channel just below the dam, gradually broadening out and dissected by numerous side channels and wooded islands. A large lake-like pool forms just above each dam.

The town of *Prairie du Chien,* is the oldest town on the Upper Mississippi River and has done much to preserve its historical past. The State Historical Society operates the elegantly restored *Villa Louis mansion,* erected by Hercules Dousman of John Astor's American Fur Company.

CR-4
FISHERMAN PARKING *(STH 82* just east of main channel bridge). Not located on water. Picnic table • grill

---

TOUR ROUTE: SOUTH OF LANSING BRIDGE, FERRYVILLE TO PRAIRIE DU CHIEN
Ferryville 5 miles• Prairie du Chien 28 miles

RUSH CREEK PUBLIC HUNTING AREA - 1700 acres just north of Ferryville are open for public duck and deer hunting and fur trapping. In recent years, buck and doe hunting have been allowed throughout the nine-day deer season.

FERRYVILLE, WISCONSIN

If this were Europe, Ferryville would be one of those tiny little burgs that are fondly remembered because you 'really got to meet the people.' The Wooden Nickel Saloon (formerly the Rattle Inn), the Swing Inn, the Grandview Motel and Neome's Motel all cling to the edge of the bluff within spittin' distance of a broad blue expanse of the Mississippi River. There's not much else to do of an evening, but chat — that is unless you hunt and fish, or enjoy boating, hiking, or photography. And of course, there are freshly made cheese curds and lightly fried catfish cheeks to be enjoyed.

Originally called *Humblebush* by its largely Norwegian settlers, the village gradually assumed the name applied to it by area farmers and commercial fishermen who gathered here to ferry their goods over to Lansing, IA, where the main fish and grain markets were located. Its tight quarters have qualified Ferryville for the Guiness Book of Records as the longest town with only a single street.

The bluffs behind the village of Ferryville are reputed to be prime rattlesnake territory. The Swing Inn has the skin of a 54" rattler on display and George, down at the Wooden Nickel Saloon, has plenty of tales to spin about close calls with his infamous neighbors, though he is quick to point out that only about ten snakes are ever seen in the area each year.

The most common rattler along the Mississippi is the *Timber rattler,* although the smaller endangered Swamp or *Massasauga rattler* can be found in wet bottomlands further north along the river. (Massasauga is a name taken from an Indian tribe found in Ontario, Canada.) In addition, the western portions of both Vernon and Crawford counties contain the only known breeding populations of *Diamondback rattlers* found east of the Mississippi. These are thought to have escaped from a circus traveling through the area near the turn of the century.

George could probably qualify as the most interesting chat in town. He has long been a licensed hunting and fishing guide. He was a snake hunter when it was still legal and he has trapped coyote, mink, fox and turtles. As everyone will tell you in these parts, the duck, turkey and deer hunting is phenomenal. It is still possible to see as many as a million ducks (local estimate) take flight and fill the sky like a swarm of gigantic insects.

CR-5
FERRYVILLE LANDING (located in village of Ferryville below the Cheese Factory). Newly-surfaced, $1 honor system launch fee.

Sugar Creek Park and baseball diamond is located at the south end of the village. Camping is allowed at no charge. New restrooms • water • no electricity

CR-6
PICNIC AREA (northeast corner of *STH 35* and *171.*) Small wayside with one table and grill.

CR-7

LARSON'S BLUFF OVERLOOK. Approximately 2 miles north of Lynxville. Follow Kettle Hollow, a gravel road, left off the Great River Road just south of CR-6. Stay to the left all the way, through a farmer's yard and continue on for another mile, plus. The view, from Lansing, IA, to the Lynxville Lock & Dam, is well worth the trouble. However, it is not well maintained or fenced. One step too far and you are **in** the Mississippi. *Indian burial mounds have been located in the vicinity, some of which are visible in the valley from Kettle Hollow road.*

CR-8

WAYSIDE (1-1/2 miles north of Lynxville). Picnic table.

CR-9

COLD SPRINGS LANDING (1 1/4 miles north of Lynxville at mouth of Cold Springs). Surfaced boat ramp. Picnic area. No water. Excellent blue gill fishing at the lower lake and near the bridge in the fall.

Traditional Quilt Block Samples

CR 6 — CR 11

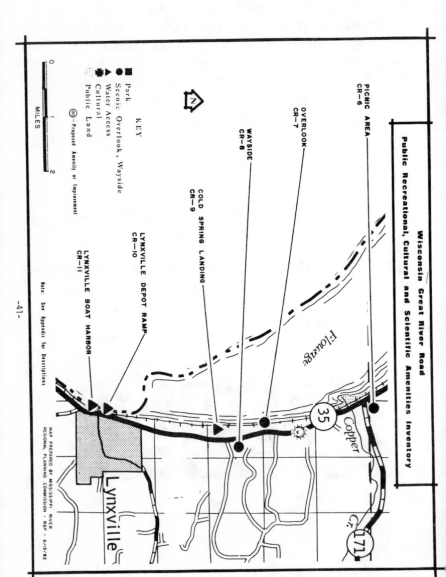

LYNXVILLE, WISCONSIN
(pop. 194)

The old railway depot is gone now, but the name remains on the boat ramp as a reminder of the days when the town numbered 2000 people. Lynxville was the major rail shipping depot in the area. Iowa farmers ferried their goods to this Wisconsin marketplace from Harpers Ferry, across the river.

A few bars, a pet corner, gas and groceries, and the local cafe along the Great River Road constitute the commercial district of this fading township. Numerous empty buildings dating from the late 19th century stare blankly out of their wooded bluffside sites — ripe, perhaps, for adoption by an enterprising artist. The old church is now an interesting collector's Antique Shop located east of Withey's Bar.

A Brief History of Lynxville

Kevin Withey is the third generation to operate the family business which began in 1908. His stories revolve around the memories of his enterprising grandfather, who was a commercial fisherman and *'market hunter.'* The market hunters were specially licensed to harvest ducks and other wildlife from the river. Their weapons were called 'punt guns' and were mounted right on the boats. They were much larger than modern guns (his grandfather's was a 4-gauge) and were loaded with anything available: shingle nails, gravel, nuts, or bolts.

The hunters might bring in their boats loaded to the water level with 500-1000 ducks. These were cleaned, packed with ice in barrels and shipped to Chicago on the train. Hunters received about 10 cents per duck.

The bulk of the population lived and farmed on numerous islands that were flooded when the lock & dams were built. The islands were heavily timbered, and along with area bluffs, provided huge rafts of lumber that were shipped south from Lynxville in the first half of this century. The demand for lumber was tremendous at this time and the dollar value of lumber to the Upper Mississippi was ultimately six times the value of the lead ore which first prompted settlement south of Cassville, WI.

Today, Lynxville (like Harpers Ferry) is largely a summer and retirement community.

RIVER HILLS ESTATES CAMPING. Very quiet, tidy RV camp with full hook-ups available. Just south of village, overlooking backwater. No showers.

CR-11
LYNXVILLE BOAT HARBOR (along *STH 35* in village). Main channel is accessible to small boats via channel from harbor under highway and railroad. Private operator. Fishing boat rentals.

CR-12
WAYSIDE AND HISTORICAL MARKER (east side of *STH 35*). Shelter and scenic river view. Marker commemorates log rafting on the Mississippi. Picnic tables • grills • water • toilets

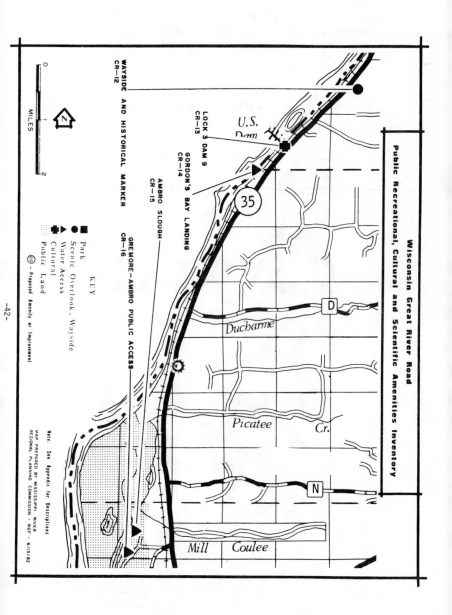

Wisconsin Great River Road
Public Recreational, Cultural and Scientific Amenities Inventory

WAYSIDE AND HISTORICAL MARKER
CR-12

LOCK 3 DAM 9
CR-13

GORDON'S BAY LANDING
CR-14

AMBRO SLOUGH
CR-15

GREMORE—AMBRO PUBLIC ACCESS
CR-16

U.S. Dam

35

Ducharme

Picatee Cr.

Mill Coulee

D

N

KEY

■ Park
● Scenic Overlook, Wayside
▲ Water Access
✦ Cultural
Public Land
⊙ – Proposed Amenity or Improvement

MILES

N

Note: See Appendix for Descriptions

MAP PREPARED BY MISSISSIPPI RIVER
REGIONAL PLANNING COMMISSION - RGF - 6/15/82

CR-13
LOCK & DAM #9. Visitor overlook to observe lock operations. Privately operated fishing float on Iowa side is accessible via ferry from Wisconsin shore. Picnic sites • toilets • water

CR-14
GORDON'S BAY LANDING. Hard surface boat landing. Picnic area • no water

Very often area farmers would simply turn their cattle, sheep, goats, pigs and other domestic animals out to graze on islands and bluffs for the summer. On occasion, animals would avoid the fall roundups and gradually become quite wild and vicious, as was the pig in this photo. The photo and article are courtesy of the Area Research Center, UW-La Crosse.

From the **LA CROSSE TRIBUNE and LEADER Press**
January 16, 1927

A wild and vicious boar of almost prehistoric size and weight, which for ten years has successfully eluded all attempts at capture and which has succeeded in keeping beyond the reach of the shells of scores of hunters, was finally shot and killed in the bottom lands below Lynxville early Thursday morning by Percy Eagon, Oakland Street, La Crosse.

The estimated weight of the animal was between 850 and 900 pounds. It was 8 feet 8 inches in length, had tusks nearly 10 inches long, and had the general build of a deer, being tall and narrow. The hunter indicated it had almost no fat and that the bristles were so wiry that it was impossible to remove them from the hide.

Farmers living in the vicinity declare that it has lived on the island opposite Lynxville for ten years or more. It was of a very vicious nature and on several occasions had treed hunters who have tried to kill it. Mr. Eagon himself has tried to kill it for a number of years, and has perched in a tree for hours at a time waiting for the animal to move on.

Eagon made the trip to the bottoms early Thursday morning with Adolph Wick and John Bridel, vowing not to come back until he had it. Within 15 minutes after their arrival, Eagon sighted it and sent a bullet into its body. The boar got to its feet and staggered into the woods but was halted by a round of shots from Bridel.

The old tusker is believed to have been the unusual offspring of escaped domestic hogs, of which there are hundreds living wild in the Winnesheik. Some of them have attained large size, but Eagon's victim is by far the largest ever known hereabouts.

In the belief that the animal may have had a mate, Frank Mader, Jacob Newberg, Ted Hanson and Matt Becker left for the bottoms this morning to hunt.

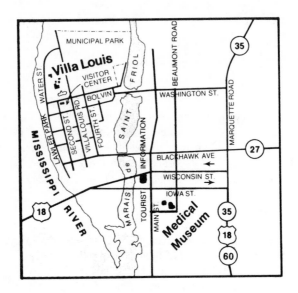

PRAIRIE DU CHIEN, WISCONSIN

Prairie du Chien, perched north of the confluence of the
Mississippi and Wisconsin rivers, had its beginnings at about
the same time that New York City was a struggling settlement
on the east coast. It is Wisconsin's second oldest town (Green
Bay is the oldest), and maintains a fairly staunch French
contingent, with Bastille Day still celebrated in July. Trans-
lated from the French, its name means *Dog Plains*. The reason
for the name is not clear though it may have referred to an
Indian chief or family with the name 'Dog.'

The French Cemetery is located on the north end of town,
near *THE BARN RESTAURANT* and the *SPORTS UNLIMITED CAMP-
GROUND*. There are 137 campsites and a pool at this resort-like
complex. Sanitary dump · electricity · sewered sites

Points of Interest

The first stop in the historic city of Prairie du Chien should be the *Wisconsin State Tourist Information Center* on *USH 18* at the foot of the bridge over the Main Channel.

CR-17
PRAIRIE DU CHIEN MARINA (On St. Feriole Island -- north of Washington St. Bridge within city limits). Hard surface ramp. 80 boat slips. Rental boats and houseboats. Marina services include gas, oil, repairs, toilets, and water.

CR-18
LA RIVIERE PARK (east side of *USH 18,* approximately one mile east of Prairie du Chien airport). Extensive city-owned open space. No formal picnic sites, no water or toilets.

CR-19
ST. FERIOLE ISLAND HISTORICAL AREA. Follow Blackhawk Avenue west to *Villa Louis,* built by the Dousman family. Today, the mansion is operated by the Wisconsin State Historical Society and is considered to be one of the finest Victorian restorations in the country. Tours daily, May 1 through October 31. Small admission fee. Its extensive grounds are open to visitors with no charge.

*The **Prairie Villa Rendezvous**, held annually during the Father's Day weekend on St. Feriole Island, is considered by modern Buckskinners to be one of the finest gatherings in the nation. Visitors can stroll around in bluejeans, tasting fried Indian breads, bartering for a bone-handled knife, touring (with permission) a voyageur's teepee or canoe campsite. No modern utensils, furnishings, or clothing are allowed for the purists in a buckskinner camp, and colorful, often scanty, Indian and frontier leather (buckskin) is the norm for participants.*

Other buildings associated with the fur trade which are open to the public include the Fur Trade Museum, the Old Dousman Hotel, picnic sites and a visitor center. Local signs direct the visitor to other historic structures and museums which are scattered throughout the city.

The old *Fort Crawford Medical Museum and Military Hospital* is located south of the State Tourist Information Center. It houses a restored pharmacy and exhibits which explain early medical/dental practices. The Military Hospital is best known for the pioneering studies of Dr. William Beaumont into the workings of the human digestive system in the 1830's. The Medical Museum is open from 10 a.m. to 5 p.m. from May 1 through October 31. Small admission fee.

The *St. Feriole Island Railroad* is located behind the Villa Grounds, along the Mississippi River banks. The restored rail cars house an assortment of shops and eateries. Visitors will enjoy relaxing on the boardwalk.

CR-20
LAWLER PARK (On St. Feriole Island). Water Street runs along the Mississippi and behind Villa Louis. Lawler City Park stretches along the river side of the street. A city beach, boat landing and the excursion paddleboat, *Prairie Bell,* are located in the park. Picnic area · riverfront walks · swimming · playground · toilets · water

CR-21
LOCKWOOD AVENUE BOAT LAUNCH (at foot of Lockwood Avenue in city). Hard surfaced ramps.

Blackhawk Avenue East takes one through the city's business district and onto Wisconsin's Great River Road, *STH 35*. Several larger shopping centers, supper clubs, and gas stations are located along *STH 35*.

PRAIRIE CAMPER SALES AND SERVICE is located on *STH 35* at the south end of town carries RV supplies.

BIG RIVER CAMPING off *STH 35*, south of town, near the Wal-Mart shopping center. Camping in a field along the water (and the railroad track) with electricity, full hook-ups.

SPECIAL EVENTS

FATHER''S DAY Weekend	Prairie du Chien, Annual *Prairie Villa Rendez-vous*. Visitors are invited to visit Buckskinner Camp held on Villa Louis grounds. Participants live, eat, sleep in style of the 1800-1850 fur traders. No charge to visitors.
Early SEPTEMBER	Prairie du Chien, Villa Louis grounds. *Carriage Classic*. Antique carriage display, trotting horse show, parade, demonstrations.

CR-17 — CR-21

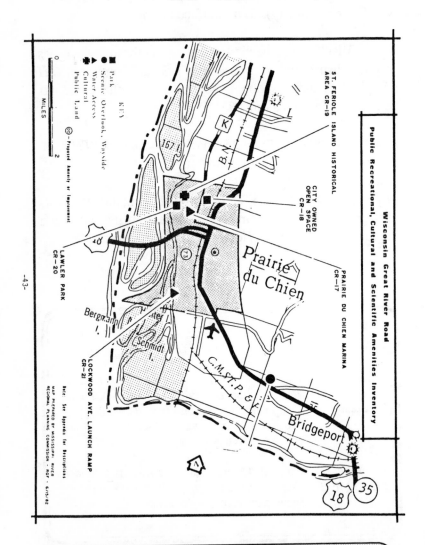

Follow *STH 35* south from Prairie du Chien toward
Cassville and Wyalusing State Park.
Stonefield Village 28 miles . Cassville 30 miles

Fur Trade

━━━━━━━━━━━━━━━━━━━━━━━━━━━━━ **161**

FUR TRADING IN PRAIRIE DU CHIEN
(AFTER 1800)
adapted from the book **Prairie du Chien** by Peter Scanlon

The first fur trading along the Upper Mississippi was probably practiced by renegade Frenchmen in the late 1500's. Duluth and Radisson in 1654 were among the earliest official emissaries of the fur trade. Radisson left the French ranks and became a charter founder of the Hudson Bay Fur Company in the 1670's.

Both licensed and unlicensed traders ("courieurs du bois" or free trappers) soon became wealthy -- Duluth retired to live in luxury in Montreal after 10 years of fur trading. The illegal trappers sold many of their pelts to Spanish buyers in Louisiana, with beaver by far the most abundant pelt.

By 1810, over 6000 French Canadians worked for Hudson Bay and the Mackinac Fur companies in the upper midwest. By 1825, over a quarter million dollars in fur was sold each year in Montreal, two thirds of which came from the American territories.

Supplying the French and Indian fur traders was big business. Indian villages, such as *Les Prairies des Chiens* which was first noted by an English explorer after 1760, often grew up around trading camps established by the fur traders. Through the trading, iron axes replaced stone; glass beads replaced quillwork; and woven cloth replaced buckskin. One ax head was worth two pelts. Iron kettles were traded for one skin per pound.

The spring and fall *Rendezvous* pulled in trappers, traders, renegades and Indians from throughout the territory. It was a time to sell pelts, resupply, socialize, drink, share news of the new government (French, English, Spanish or American) and boast of exploits in the wilderness.

In October 1824 the American Fur Co. in New York City had the greatest quantity of furs ever offered at auction. There were 12,500 lbs. of beaver pelts, 120,000 lbs. of muskrat pelts, 72,000 racoon pelts, and 10,000 buffalo robes. In 1827, John Jacob Astor sold partly by auction and partly by private sale 550,000 muskrat skins at an average of 36 cents apiece.

Astor's son once estimated the annual income of the company as $500,000. It's been estimated that in 10 years of business at St. Louis, the Astor company (American Fur) made more than one million dollars. In all, the fur business netted Astor between one and two million dollars.

Hercules Dousman arrived in Prairie du Chien as an agent of the company in 1826. In 1834 he became a significant owner in the American Fur Company, supplying traders established along the northern length of the river. Many of today's river towns are located at Dousman's supply points. Dousman reinvested much of his profits into the midwest, while Astor's profits went to New York.

The transplanting of the Indians after the Black Hawk War, and their final removal in 1848 brought the local fur trade to an end. When furs became scarce in Prairie du Chien, northern Minnesota became the next center of fur trading. In 1848, Dousman and his partner sold out to Henry Hastings Sibley in St. Paul and ended the company's presence in Prairie du Chien.

Wisconsin's Oldest County

GRANT COUNTY

In Grant County, the Great River Road leaves behind busy, modern State Highway 35 and begins a rural meandering along well maintained county highways on its way to the historic *lead mining* area of Wisconsin's southwestern corner. Several state parks are found within this area, including *Wyalusing, Nelson Dewey,* and *First Capitol* state parks and *Stonefield Village State Historic Site.*

Grant County, the southernmost Wisconsin county along Wisconsin's Great River Road, is rich in history as well as scenery. John Wilkes Booth supposedly entertained miners in a theater in *Tennyson* and the oldest cemetery in Wisconsin is at *British Hollow* where many veterans of the Black Hawk War are buried.

It is believed that Nicholas Perrot discovered the first Indian lead mine in 1690 at Snake Cave (St. John's Mine) in *Potosi.* During the lead mining era of the 1820's, 10,000 mines were located in Grant County, and it was not until 1846 that Milwaukee surpassed Potosi as the largest township in the new state. The small village of *Belmont* just west of Platteville in Lafayette County was designated as Wisconsin's first capital.

Two excellent fishing and canoeing rivers, the *Grant* and *Platte rivers,* meander south through rolling farmland and scenic rock outcroppings to enter the Mississippi at Potosi. Shuttle services are available at Burton and Potosi. *Canoe rentals* and shuttle service on the *Wisconsin River* are available in Bagley.

As an alternate route, follow *USH 151* northeast of *Dickeyville* and Grant County toward *Dodgeville. Belmont Mound State Park* is the highest point in Southern Wisconsin and has picnicking and playground facilities. *Platteville* is home to the *Chicago Bears* training camp in August. Several museums and mining tours for the traveler are available in town. *Mineral Point* is a surprise even to most Wisconsinites. The State Historical Society operates *Pendarvis,* the old Cornish miner's home dating from the 1830's while several private antique shops and bookstores are housed in *Shake Rag Alley.*

Front Street painted by Marion Biehn.

SPECIAL EVENTS

DECEMBER	Stonefield village, west of Cassville. *Christmas celebration* with period decorations, sleigh rides.
Early JUNE	Annual *Cassville Women's Club Tea* at Stonefield. Free refreshments, entertainment provided by costumed members at the Dewey Mansion. Regular admission fee.
JULY 4th Weekend	Mineral Point. Annual *Pendarvis Quilt Show*. Exhibition of old and new quilts from the Historical Society collection and those private collections.
JULY	*Cassville TWIN-O-RAMA*. National celebration/reunion honoring biological twins. Held annually for over 40 years. Food, beverages, contests, parade. Venetian boat parade. Carnival. Special programming during the three-day event.
JULY	*Shakespeare Festival in Platteville*. A month of excellent Shakespearean drama at the University of Wisconsin, Platteville.
AUGUST 2nd weekend	Potosi-Tennyson. *Annual Catfish Festival*. Also Tri-State Scout Powwow. 4.2 mile run, catfish dinners.

> ## TOUR ROUTE: WYALUSING TO POTOSI
>
> The Great River Road follows *STH 35* south from Prairie du Chien to Bloomington, WI, then south on *STH 133* to Cassville, WI. The route which follows assumes a visit to Wyalusing State Park then continues south on *CTH X* toward Cassville.

GR-1
WYALUSING STATE PARK (on *CTH C*, 4 miles west of *Ush 18)*. State Park on bluffs towering over the confluence of Wisconsin and Mississippi Rivers. Excellent *camping* with electricity at some sites. Dump station. Hard surfaced boat landing at Glen Lake, within the park, gives access to the Mississippi. Picnicking • playground • hiking • Indian Mounds • scientific areas

Striking view of the Wisconsin River flowing into the Mississippi from *Lookout Point*. Marker commemorates July 17, 1673, when Fr. James Marquette and Louis Joliet first looked upon the vast Mississippi "with great joy." Many of the great influx of immigrants in the 1860's who had traveled up the Mississippi from St. Louis, continued north on the Wisconsin to settle in central Wisconsin.

GR-2
WYALUSING RECREATION AREA (north edge of tiny village of Wyalusing on *CTH X)*. Large river beach and hard surfaced boat ramp. Shelter • picnicking • water

VILLAGE OF WYALUSING. Tiny settlement of several houses of native stone and a church perched just south and slightly up the bluff from the recreation site. Originally populated by 19 riverboat pilots (who, no doubt, chose the lovliest spot on the river!).

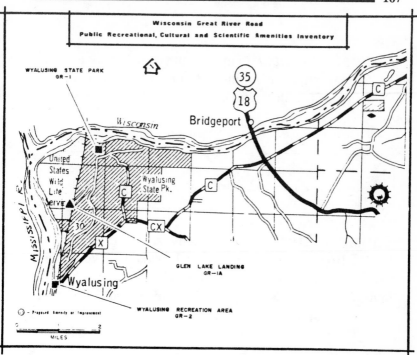

Wisconsin Great River Road
Public Recreational, Cultural and Scientific Amenities Inventory

WYALUSING STATE PARK
GR-1

Wisconsin

Bridgeport

United States Wild Life Reserve

Wyalusing State Pk.

GLEN LAKE LANDING
GR-1A

MISSISSIPPI R.

Wyalusing

○ - Proposed Amenity or Improvement

WYALUSING RECREATION AREA
GR-2

0   2
MILES

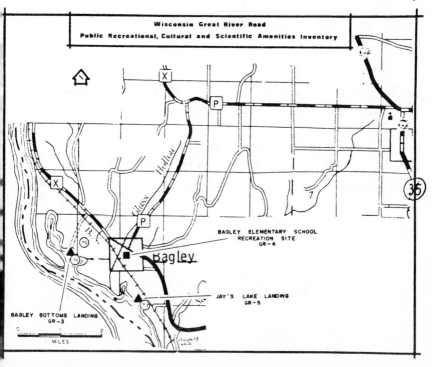

Wisconsin Great River Road
Public Recreational, Cultural and Scientific Amenities Inventory

BAGLEY ELEMENTARY SCHOOL
RECREATION SITE
GR-4

Bagley

Glass Hollow

JAY'S LAKE LANDING
GR-5

BAGLEY BOTTOMS LANDING
GR-3

0   2
MILES

GR-3

WAYNE'S CAMPGROUND (3 miles south of state park on *CTH X*).   {} **Overnight camping**, $3.   Quiet, just off roadside. Camping is $6 with electricity.

> **Follow *CTH A* south from Bagley, then on *CTH VV* to Nelson Dewey State Park and the village of Cassville**

JELLYSTONE CAMPGROUND (directly across from road to Bagley Bottoms on east side, well marked). Well-maintained, full hook-up campground with activity schedule. Invites *day use* for $2 a person. Swimming pool • miniature golf • camp store

GR-4

BAGLEY SCHOOL RECREATION SITE (Walnut St., in village). Serves as Village Park. Picnic tables • playground• not on waterfront

VILLAGE OF BAGLEY. Bagley Hotel has 7 rooms, air conditioned. Supper Club, cocktail lounge.

NOTE: Mystery buffs may be interested in the case of Charlie Ross, who is buried in the Bagley cemetery. Kidnapped from a wealthy Pennsylvania family in the 1920's and found barely alive in one of the boat houses in Bagley. He died before being reunited with his family who had already depleted most of their resources in searching for him. His kidnapper was never discovered. His story was told in the book entitled simply, "Charlie Ross."

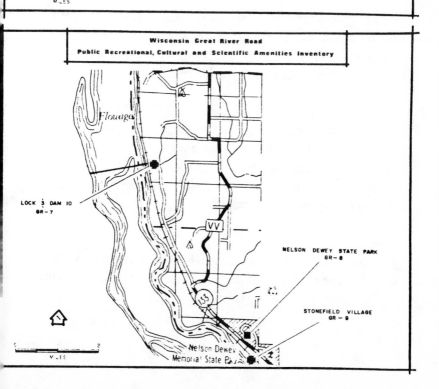

Wisconsin Great River Road
Public Recreational, Cultural and Scientific Amenities Inventory

GLENHAVEN RECREATION AREA
GR-6

Glenhaven

MILES

Wisconsin Great River Road
Public Recreational, Cultural and Scientific Amenities Inventory

Flowage

LOCK & DAM 10
GR-7

NELSON DEWEY STATE PARK
GR-8

STONEFIELD VILLAGE
GR-9

Nelson Dewey
Memorial State Park

MILES

GR-5
RIVER OF LAKES CAMPGROUND (just south of Bagley, well marked.) Privately owned cabins, marina, 120 campsites with full hook-ups. River beach in campground • camp store • boat rental • playground

JAY'S LAKE LANDING (south of Bagley). Hard surfaced ramp • picnicking • no water

GR-6
GLEN HAVEN RECREATION AREA (in village of Glen Haven). Hard surfaced ramp • picnicking • no water

GR-7
LOCK & DAM #10. Toe end only. Operating and viewing facilities are in Guttenberg, IA.

The drive to Nelson Dewey State Park along CTH VV passes through a deep hollow, heavily wooded and sparsely populated. Very pretty. Road is in very good condition, but winding, so plan this for leisurely travel.

EAGLE VALLEY NATURE PRESERVE is located about 6 miles north of Stonefield Village. Watch for Duncan Road sign off *CTH VV* and follow west and north, 1 mile, to the preserve. Excellent observation point for migrating and wintering bald eagles. Almost 1000 eagles are counted here during the January eagle counts.

GR-8
NELSON DEWEY STATE PARK (1 mile north of Village of Cassville on *CTH VV*). State park on bluffs along the

river. No formal boat launch area. Indian mounds are easily accessible by car and well marked. Park commemorates the home area of Wisconsin's first governor. Extensive picnic area and excellent camping with gravel pads in wooded sites. Electricity • dump station

GR-9
STONEFIELD VILLAGE (in Nelson Dewey State Park). This replica of typical 1800's village offers the sights, sounds and smells of life in a rural settlement before the turn of the century. Special Christmas displays with horse drawn sleigh rides. School house, bird sanctuary. Admission fee.

NELSON DEWEY ESTATE (east side of road, just south of State Park). Guided tours of the Nelson Dewey Home.

VILLAGE OF CASSVILLE. 4 Supper Clubs, 1 cafe. Drive-in at Crawford and Front St. near the village park. Several motels and resorts are advertised in the area, some with camping. Cassville is the site of the national *Twin-O-Rama* held for three days in July. Competitions • parade • Chicken-Q • carnival and Venetian parade

GR-10
CASSVILLE SWIMMING POOL PARK (north end of village, along road). Small fee. Large pool • playground • tennis courts

GR-11
CASSVILLE MISSISSIPPI RIVER FERRY. The automobile ferry between Cassville and Guttenberg, IA, offers the traveler a unique river experience. There are no bridges which cross the river to Iowa until the bridge at Dickeyville.

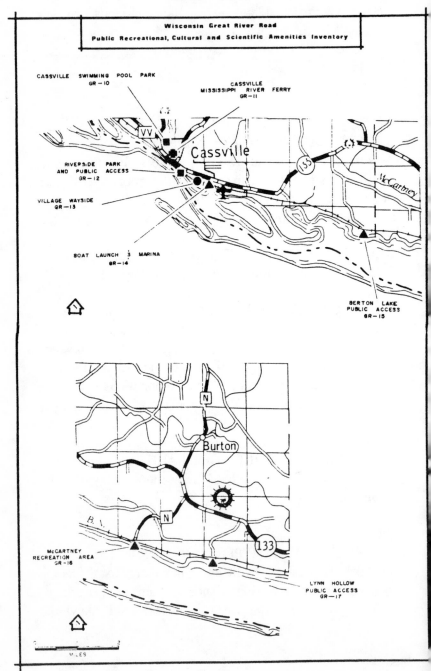

Wisconsin Great River Road
Public Recreational, Cultural and Scientific Amenities Inventory

CASSVILLE SWIMMING POOL PARK
GR-10

CASSVILLE
MISSISSIPPI RIVER FERRY
GR-11

Cassville

RIVERSIDE PARK
AND PUBLIC ACCESS
GR-12

VILLAGE WAYSIDE
GR-13

McCartney

BOAT LAUNCH & MARINA
GR-14

BERTON LAKE
PUBLIC ACCESS
GR-15

Burton

McCARTNEY
RECREATION AREA
GR-16

LYNN HOLLOW
PUBLIC ACCESS
GR-17

MILES

GR-12
RIVERSIDE PARK AND PUBLIC BOAT ACCESS (Front
Street in Cassville, west of *STH 133*). Well developed park
with two boat ramps.   Picnicking • shelter houses • playground • toilets • water

*The Mississippi River was the 'Main Street' of every
river town. Almost every town has its Front Street running
along the river. This was the 'river business' street in a town,
replete with docks, warehouses, and offices. These river
front streets usually make an interesting drive as the oldest
commercial buildings are often found here.*

*Community riverfronts are gradually being devel-
oped into prime park and business locations. Well developed, they become an enticing invitation to pleasure boaters
to make a visit to town.*

The Great River Road now follows *STH 133* south to Potosi, WI

GR-13
VILLAGE WAYSIDE (south of village of Cassville). No
river access. Picnicking • water • toilets

GR-14
BOAT LAUNCH AND MARINA (Jack Oak Road on south
side of Village). Privately operated as *Eagles Roost Motel
and Cabins*. Hard surfaced boat ramp.

GR-15
BURTOM LAKE PUBLIC ACCESS (3 miles south of
Cassville on Fur-Nuf Rd. west of *STH 133*). Non-surfaced
local boat landing. 8 ' 4 " overhead clearance.

GR-16

MC CARTNEY RECREATION AREA *(CTH N* west of *STH 133* between Cassville and village of Potosi at mouth of McCartney Creek). Small hard surfaced ramp with access to Mississippi. Excellent bluegill fishing in season. Three miles off the Great River Road and a long, steep winding descent to river level. Small park. Picnicking • no water or toilets

GR-17

LYNN HOLLOW PUBLIC ACCESS (Lynn Hollow Road, west of *STH 133).* Steep, winding descent to non-surfaced ramp.

GR-18

POTOSI RECREATION AREA (West side of Potosi on River and *STH 133).* Concrete plank ramp. Located on peninsula in river.

The venerable Delta Queen pulls into riverside park.

THE PORT OF POTOSI

The adjacent villages of Potosi and Tennyson (originally Snake Hollow and Dutch Hollow) lay at the heart of the lead mining region of Southwestern Wisconsin. The name "Potosi" is an old Pueblo Indian word meaning mineral wealth and was aptly applied to this 'lead rush' settlement. St. John's Mine, located along the Great River Road in Potosi, offers a tour of an authentic hand-dug lead mine. It is also the starting point of a self-guided tour of the historical township. The tour is based on the yellow and brown triangular signs posted throughout the township.

There is likely to be no problem finding your way in Potosi as the three-mile-long Main Street is the only street in town. Several supper clubs, cafes and stores are located at the top of the hill in adjacent Tennyson.

St. John's mine was originally called Snake Cave and was discovered in 1690 by Nicholas Perrot. Before that time, Indians were chipping out lead crystals for decoration and to trade with the French trappers and traders in the valley. It was the lead mining regions of southwestern Wisconsin that provided all of the lead used by Northern troops (and most of that used by Southern troops) in the Civil War. Local history suggests that Jefferson Davis bought over one million dollars worth of lead in this area one year before the war began.

Closed in 1879, it was not opened again until 1975. Many of the mining artifacts discovered then are on display during the guided tour. While the tour is highly recommended at all times, it is a real treat when it is 93 degrees outside and 56 degrees *inside* the mine.

Note the 'shingle art' in the roof of the St. John Mine office. The letters P-E-A-C-E are arranged across the top of the roof. Can you also see Chief Winnebago or an Eagle in the main shingle design?

Potosi was the leading port on the upper Mississippi from 1836 to 1848. Not only were 'pigs' of lead being shipped out on the steamboats, but lumber from the Kickapoo and Wisconsin rivers was rafted and shipped and Potosi was the main agricultural port for the farmers in southwestern Wisconsin. All the river towns and tradings posts all the way to Fort Snelling in Minnesota picked up supplies here. In 1845, Potosi was the largest town in western Wisconsin.

Meanwhile, the Grant River was steadily silting in the port area and despite efforts to maintain the port, by 1850 Cassville had become the major port on the Mississippi.

The real death knell for western Wisconsin's most important port city came, however, in 1849 with the California Gold Rush. The promise of greater riches than lead could offer lured away the bulk of Potosi's mining community, paralyzing local trade and industry.

Across the river, the village of Dubuque seized upon the vagaries of fate and became the metropolitan area that it was once thought Potosi would ultimately become.

GR-19
WAYSIDE (south of Potosi, approximately 1-1/2 miles on south side of *STH 133)*. Shelter • picnicking • water • toilets • grills

GR-20
PLATTE RIVER ACCESS (On *USH 61-STH 133* crossing the Platte River). Not a developed landing, but useable for small boats and canoes. Launch point is approximately 3-1/2 miles above the Platte River mouth into the Mississippi.

GR-21
GRANT RIVER RECREATION AREA (approximately 2 miles southwest of *USH 61-STH 35* at Potosi. Well marked.) Well developed, Corps of Engineers maintained campground. 73 sites with electricity, water and 10 walk-in tent camping sites. Senior Citizens 50% off. Hot showers • toilets • picnicking

GR-22
SOUTH POTOSI BOAT LAUNCH (1/2 mile south of *Grant River Recreation area)*. No water or toilets.

GR-23
BANFIELD BRIDGE PUBLIC ACCESS (Platte River — west of Banfield Road from *USH 61-STH 35* between Potosi and Dickeyville). Non-surfaced ramp. Access to site is difficult.

DICKEYVILLE, WISCONSIN. Motels, restaurants. Highways 61, 35, and 151 all converge in Dickeyville. Named after the town's first grocer, Dickeyville was started as a German farming community in the late 1880's.

WISCONSIN'S 'OLD COPPER CULTURE'

Archeological digs have been ongoing in the Potosi area since 1945. Radiocarbon dating of relics found in the area indicate that Indians of the Old Copper Culture were well established along the river from before 2710 B.C. until about the time of Christ. These people were food gatherers and hunters. From about 1000 B.C. to the coming of the white man in the 1600's, the Woodland Cultures occupied this area.

The Woodland Indians were among the well-known "Mound Builders." It is believed that these mounds, which may or may not have been burial mounds, once covered much of Wisconsin. Most have disappeared with mining and the farmer's plow. A very few do remain preserved and visible at various parks and monuments along the river.

GR-24
DICKEYVILLE COMMUNITY PARK (North side of village on *USH 151*). Not located on river. Shelter • picnicking • grills • playground

GR-25
DICKEYVILLE GROTTO (in village, on *USH 61-STH 35*). A privately owned site. Unique shrine constructed of bits of stone, glass and shells by Father Mathias Wernerus in honor of his God and country. Picnicking • no water.

Follow *USH 151 - 61* south across the bridge into Dubuque, Iowa.

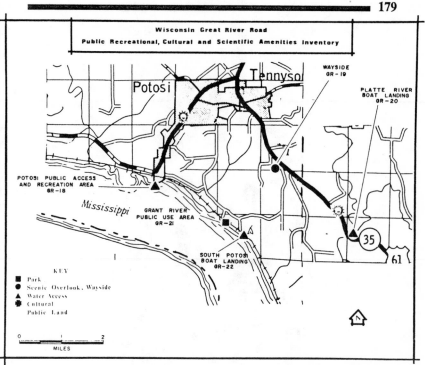

Wisconsin Great River Road
Public Recreational, Cultural and Scientific Amenities Inventory

Potosi

Tennyson

WAYSIDE
GR – 19

PLATTE RIVER
BOAT LANDING
GR – 20

POTOSI PUBLIC ACCESS
AND RECREATION AREA
GR – 18

Mississippi

GRANT RIVER
PUBLIC USE AREA
GR – 21

SOUTH POTOSI
BOAT LANDING
GR – 22

35

61

KEY
■ Park
● Scenic Overlook, Wayside
▲ Water Access
✦ Cultural
Public Land

0   1   2
MILES

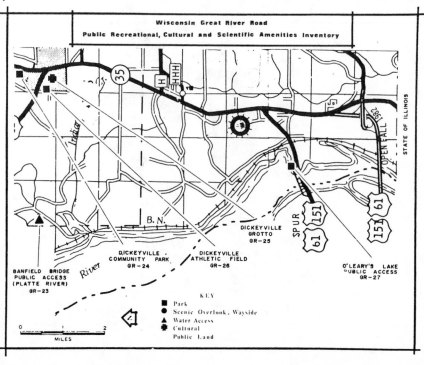

Wisconsin Great River Road
Public Recreational, Cultural and Scientific Amenities Inventory

35

Indian

STATE OF ILLINOIS

OPEN FALL 1982

151

61

61
SPUR

151
61

B. N.

River

DICKEYVILLE
GROTTO
GR – 25

DICKEYVILLE
COMMUNITY PARK
GR – 24

DICKEYVILLE
ATHLETIC FIELD
GR – 26

O'LEARY'S LAKE
PUBLIC ACCESS
GR – 27

BANFIELD BRIDGE
PUBLIC ACCESS
(PLATTE RIVER)
GR – 23

KEY
■ Park
● Scenic Overlook, Wayside
▲ Water Access
✦ Cultural
Public Land

0   1   2
MILES

Upper Mississippi River Fur Trader

Old Beginnings

DUBUQUE, IOWA
AND
GALENA, ILLINOIS

From Dickeyville, WI, America's Great River Road follows *USH 61-151* south onto *USH 20* to the restored, picture-book city of Galena, IL, the destination of this Guide. The Great River Road then continues through Illinois and Iowa, to St. Louis, MO, and the Gulf of Mexico.

Also included here is the city of Dubuque, IA, whose history, like that of Galena, is intimately intertwined with the rest of the old Wisconsin Territory. In fact, both Dubuque and Galena (as well as Chicago) were added to the Illinois territory only after it became questionable whether there were enough votes to make Illinois a free (non-slave) state.

STH 61-151 leads directly over the Mississippi River and into Dubuque. The *Greyhound Racing Park, Riverview Park* and the *Dubuque Yacht Basin* of modern Dubuque glisten below the highway. The *Clock Tower* and gold-domed roof of the *County Courthouse* beckon the traveler into historic Dubuque.

The visitor from Chicago and Galena, IL, on *USH 20*, will enjoy the panoramic view from the bridge over the Mississippi. The exit for the *Port of Dubuque Iowa Welcome Center* and *Ice Harbor* is well marked and deposits the visitor at the doorstep of Iowa's newest and largest Welcome Center (open April 1991). Located in the renovated Diamond Jo Warehouse, the center offers Iowa tourism information and an Iowa products gift shop. The *National Rivers Hall of Fame* is located on the 2nd floor and the *Dubuque Heritage Museum* is located on the 3rd floor.

The fourth floor observation area offers views to the north of the *Shot Tower* (used to produce lead shot during the Civil War) and the Zele Brewing Company; to the east, the Mississippi River's main channel; to the south, the Ice Harbor; and to the west, *St. Raphael's Cathedral,* the bluffs, and the *Fenelon Place Elevator.* Adjacent to the building is the *Dubuque Casino Belle,* the largest riverboat gambling casino on the Mississippi River.

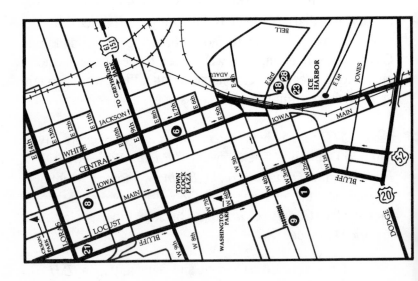

City of Dubuque, IA

What to See in Dubuque (Keyed to City map)

THE ICE HARBOR was built by the Army Corps of Engineers in the mid-1880's to shelter boats over-wintering in Dubuque. The Harbor hums with the coming and going of tour busses, and one or more of the colorful paddlewheelers of **Roberts River Rides** churn eagerly at the dock. The *Mississippi Belle* is a huge excursion boat with two elegant dining floors, two upper decks, five bars, and fifty employees catering to 600 to 800 passengers daily. For details on casino gambling and the *Dubuque Casino Belle,* please see Appendix, page 211.

THE WOODWARD RIVERBOAT MUSEUM (28) is one of the finest historical museums along the river and offers an extensive collection of regional books. Three dimensional, hands-on displays bring to life the diverse elements that together have formed the fabric of life along the Mississippi during the past 300 years: Indians, fur traders, lead mining, the steamboats, logging, clamming, and the natural scenic beauty of the Mississippi River gorge.

The Riverboat Museum ticket is also good for admittance to the *Sidewheeler William M. Black Museum* (23), the largest dredge boat to work the Mississippi River, and the displays of the *National Rivers Hall of Fame* (18) located in the Iowa Welcome Center.

EAGLE POINT PARK (164 acres located on west Shiras Avenue.) A beautiful park with scenic overlooks of the river and Lock & Dam #11. Picnic tables·playgrounds·stone shelters · tennis courts

The *Tollbridge Restaurant,* directly below Eagle Point Park at the west end of Rhomberg Avenue, offers diners a similar scenic backdrop. Built atop an old bridge foundation, it is a comfortable perch for winter eagle watching!

CATHEDRAL SQUARE (1), on Bluff Street between 1st and 2nd streets. St. Raphael Cathedral, built between 1857 and 1859, presides over this small park area. The beautiful stonework, tracery windows and arches are done in the *Gothic Revival* style. The interior frescoing was done under the direction of Italian artist, Gregori. The Church contains the bones of a young Christian martyr killed in the amphitheaters of Rome.

ST. LUKE'S United Methodist Church (12th & Main) boasts over 110 Tiffany stained glass windows. A sole non-Tiffany window, seen upon entering the sanctuary, provides a clear contrast to Tiffany's windows seen throughout the building.

FENELON SQUARE ELEVATOR (9) or Tramway climbs 189 feet to the top of a 300 foot bluff overlooking the Ice Harbor. Built in 1882 by a local banker who desired to speed his trip home to the top of the bluff, the inclined railway is one of only three such cable cars in the nation. The cable was produced by the builder of the Brooklyn Bridge and turnstiles were purchased from the Chicago Exposition. Today a round trip is $1. From the summit on Fenelon Place there is an unobstructed view over the harbor, the Mississippi River, and three states.

Fenelon Place was one of the most prestigious residential areas of Dubuque in the mid-19th century. It was the bankers, architects, lead, and logging magnates who built homes here. The sturdy, square *Georgian Revival* style was prominent and excellent examples can be seen at 710 and 732 Fenelon. Several guides to Dubuque's historic architecture are available at the Riverboat Museum.

CABLE CAR SQUARE AND SHOPS (9) and HARBOR PLACE MALL at the Ice Harbor offer fine arts, crafts, pottery, stained glass, antiques, china, and clothing.

The OLD SHOT TOWER (22) is visible from the Cable Car Summit. Built on the waterfront next to the railroad bridge in 1856, it produced lead shot during the Civil War. The neighboring Zele Brewery opens its taste-testing rooms from 11 a.m. to 6 p.m. daily except Monday.

DUBUQUE MUSEUM OF ART/OLD JAIL AND COUNTY COURT-HOUSE (6). The golden dome of the County Courthouse tops a stately building built in 1893. The neighboring jail is built in a rare *Egyptian Revival* style. Both structures are on the National Register of Historic Places. The art museum is closed Mondays.

The GREYHOUND RACING TRACK is well signed. Be aware of numerous one-way streets. Follow 9th street out onto the island where the Greyhound Park and the Dubuque Yacht Basin are located. Campers will enjoy *Riverview Park and Campground* which is directly beyond the Greyhound Park and left along the river. It is right on the river with no railroad tracks nearby. **No swimming,** please, as the undertow is dangerous. Picnic tables · grills · electricity · water

THE HERITAGE BIKING TRAIL runs between Dubuque and Dyersville, IA. Seasonal opportunities for hiking, biking, skiing, snowmobiling, and nature study on a converted railbed. The 26 mile long trail is fairly level and is accented by rock outcroppings and meandering streams.

MINES OF SPAIN RECREATION AREA (accessible from *STH 52)*. 1380-acre area managed by the Iowa Dept. of Natural Resources. *E.B. Lyons Nature Center* displays area fossils, wildlife, eagle's nest, and live rattlesnake. The *Julien Dubuque Monument* is located in the recreation area as are hiking trails, lead mining pits, and Indian mounds. Listed on the National Register of Historic Places.

SPECIAL EVENTS

Mid-June	The *Great Mississippi Sailboat Race*. The race from Bellevue, to Dubuque, IA, is the longest race on the Mississippi.
July 4	*Mathias Ham House Ice Cream Social*. Lincoln Ave., Dubuque. Food, Beverages and Historic Interpretation.
3rd Weekend in May	*DubuqueFest* All-Arts Festival. Juried arts and Crafts fair, dance drama, House Tours, ethnic food, more.
1st Sunday in August	*Craft Fair at Washington Park*. 6th and Locust Streets, Dubuque.
September	*Riverfest*. Dubuque Ice Harbor. Focus on River History, activities. Parade, arts, crafts, beer garden, Venetian Parade.

A Bit of Dubuque History

Julien Dubuque secured a claim to the lead rich area of present-day Dubuque from the Spanish in 1790, long before the Galena lead rush peaked in 1830. Julien, who originally worked the area as a fur trader, eventually developed the *Spanish Lead Mines* with his Indian wife.

Dubuque died before the steamboat was invented, however, so was never able to ship out highly profitable quantities of the mineral. With the area under complete Indian control, there was no further lead mining until the late 1820's, after the *Virginia* became the first steamboat to travel clear north to Fort Snelling. The 1820's were boom days in the frontier town of Galena and by 1833 present-day Iowa was opened to settlement. In 1837 the Territorial Government of Wisconsin permitted the village of Dubuque to incorporate.

As the prosperity of the lead mines declined, agriculture began to flourish. Flour and grist mills, the railways and lumbering industries each made their mark on the county.

During the mid-19th century, excursions into the scenic upper Mississippi provided an important source of riverboat income. Tourists as well as settlers were flocking upriver. A journal entry from 1830 notes:

"Tourists swarm to the Mississippi River, as well as immigrants. Here are thrown together people of every country and every character. You may see one day English, Irish, German, French, Swiss, Indian, fur trader and Americans, and in such a variety of national customs and costumes as is rarely to be found, in any other place."

The Diamond Jo Steamboat Line, headquartered in Dubuque, was founded by "Diamond Joe" Reynolds in 1862. It eventually became one of the largest packet companies on the Mississippi River carrying freight and passengers.

Galena, Rock Island, and La Crosse were also major ports at this time. Dubuque recorded one thousand steamboat landings in 1857. After the 1850's, however, the railroads started to ply the river banks and soon snatched the bulk of the freight and passenger service from the steamboats.

CAMPGROUNDS IN THE GALENA/DUBUQUE AREA

Dubuque Yacht Basin RV Park — 16th Street and the River. Across from the Greyhound Park. Electricity, showers, swimming pool, laundry, convenience store, game room. Shuttle to Dog Park. (319) 556-7708

Mud Lake Marina — 6 miles north of Dubuque. Fishing, camping, electricity. 319-552-2746

Palace Campground — 1 mile west of Galena on *USH 20*. Camping, swimming pool, full hook-ups and showers. (815) 777-2466

Riverview Park Campgrounds — Off Kerper Blvd. in Dubuque. Just beyond the Greyhound Park and left along the river. Some electricity. Directly on the river, no railroad nearby. Boating, playground, fishing. (319) 582-5775

Rustic Barn Campground — 3854 Dry Hollow Road, Kieler, WI, just off *USH 61-151* south of Dickeyville, WI.

TOUR ROUTE: DUBUQUE, IA, TO GALENA, IL
15 miles to Galena on *USH 20*

GALENA, ILLINOIS

The familiar Pilot's Wheel of America's Great River Road greets the traveler again on *USH 20* east out of Dubuque and toward Galena, IL. The road heads inland from East Dubuque into the rolling, agriculture-rich hills of Jo Daviess

County. Just north of Galena, one begins to notice the flavor of the southern cultural traditions fostered by Galena's close ties with the Mississippi river and communities down river. The colorful county name commemorates a Kentucky hero of the Civil War days. The name was chosen despite the local constituency by the overwhelming majority in the state house who had Kentucky roots.

These southern symphathies almost put Illinois on the side of the south during the Civil War. It was not until the coming of the railroads and the influx of Yankee farmers and businessmen that loyalties became widely focused on the northeast.

A Bit of Galena History

Galena's glory days came early and faded quickly with all the intensity of California's gold rush days. It was known since the 1680's that great deposits of lead were mined by the Indians to trade for European goods, but it was not until 1819 that a boatload of 100 men came to establish a commercial effort in what was then known as the Fever River.

In 1823, the *Virginia,* the army's first steamboat to reach Fort Snelling in St. Paul, docked at the camp. It was the steamboat that made all the difference to Galena. Lead could now be shipped out in great (and heavy) quantity. In 1825 there may have been 200 people in the area — by 1828 there were somewhere between 5000 and 10,000 hardy souls. The boom days were on!

The commercial district prospered as farmers and miners ventured out from Galena, returning for supplies and to ship out produce. Many valley towns, such as Cassville,

Platteville, Mineral Point, Genoa, WI, and Winona, MN, were established by prospectors and entrepreneurs based in Galena.

The Civil War ripped through the country in 1865 and Galena had its last burst of national reknown. In an ironic twist of fate, eight Union generals came from Galena. One of them, Ulysses S. Grant, rose to command the Union Army and accept the surrender of Gen. Robert E. Lee. In 1868, Grant became the 18th President of the United States.

By 1870, Galena's lead production was no longer nationally significant. Much of the population had followed the Gold Rush west or filtered north into Wisconsin, Iowa and Minnesota. The railroads by-passed this steamboat port, laying track directly from Chicago to Prairie du Chien and La Crosse. As steamboat traffic faded, the Galena River sediment began silting in the Galena River so that today it (like the town it served) is only a pretty shadow of its former self.

The Ryan House greets visitors arriving in Galena from the north.

What to See in Galena

Galena, today, is an architectural pastry. The commercial district built to serve the needs of 10,000 people 100 years ago remains almost completely intact. There has been little need for a population which ranged from 3000 in the 1930's to almost 7000 today to construct anything new.

The two major streets, Main and Bench (which is terraced up the hill above Main) are lined with commercial and public buildings dating from as early as the 1830's. Private homes, built to reflect the great wealth generated during the lead mining days, dot the hills throughout the village.

Galena's beautiful Victorian homes date mainly from the 1850's to the 1870's. In comparison, the historic homes in most towns up river will date from the 1880's to the 1900's. The *Ryan House*, *The Belvidere House*, and *Stillman's Country Inn* are just samples of the many elegant mansions built during the mid-19th century boom days.

Guided tours are available in several of the homes, including Grant's home. Many others are open to the public as guest homes and Bed and Breakfast Inns. A complete list of lodging (including prices) is available from the *Visitor's Center, 101 Bouthillier St., Galena, IL 61036*. A printed *architectural walking tour* of the village is also available free from the center. The Spring and Fall Home Tours are among the most popular annual events in town.

Plan to treat yourself well during your stop in Galena. More than 25 antique shops and seemingly endless specialty boutiques are located in this town which is a shopper's dream. The *Truffles Restaurant* at the newly restored *DeSoto Hotel* offers fine dining in a quiet, sunlit interior courtyard. *Pete's Steak House* and *Clark's Restaurant* are local favorites for good home cooking. The ice cream shop promises homemade sugar cones, hot fudge, and old fashioned malts — all accompanied by a merry player piano.

Points of Interest

A first stop in Galena might be the *Visitor's Center* located in the old railroad depot. Those arriving on *USH 20* from the west would cross the bridge over the Galena river and turn left. The Center is well marked. *Grant Park* is a major city park located just down the street from the Visitor Center. This beautiful city park offers picnicking, playground and a picturesque view of the old town of Galena.

The picturesque, working *flood gates* of the commercial district protect the downtown area against flooding of the river as well as torrents of water which wash down *USH 20* during storms.

The OLD MARKET HOUSE on Commerce and Perry Streets is operated by the Illinois Historic Preservation Agency. The Main Hall has an *architectural exhibit* which helps the visitor recognize the many styles of Galena's buildings.

The *COUNTY HISTORICAL MUSEUM* is located at 211 S. Bench Street. An excellent slide show on the history of Jo Daviess County is presented regularly through the day. Exhibits detail life during the lead mining and Civil War days. Nast's famous life size painting of Lee's Surrender to Gen. Grant fills one wall. Small fee.

The DESOTO HOUSE was built in 1855 for the grand price of $85,000. It had five stories, more than 200 rooms and was furnished with velvet carpets, rosewood furniture, satin curtains, intricately carved wood accents, marble table tops and statuary. Horace Greeley, James Russell Lowell, and Abraham Lincoln all stayed at the DeSoto. It formed the headquarters for Grant's presidential campaign. Today it has been elegantly restored and has several interesting shops which line the courtyard of the Truffles Restaurant.

GRACE EPISCOPAL CHURCH is located on Hill and Prospect Streets. It was built in 1847 to replace the frame

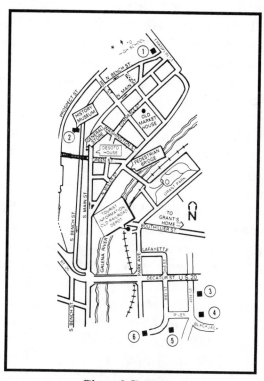

City of Galena

chapel built in 1838. Its stained glass windows came from Belgium. Its organ, the first brought to the Northwest, was shipped to New Orleans from Philadelphia by sailing boat and then up the river on a steamboat.

The FIRST PRESBYTERIAN CHURCH, built in 1838, is just down the block. According to Galena history, it was founded by a Yale and Princeton graduate who had appealed to the American Missionary Society for an assignment so difficult "that no one else will take it." During the 1840's, his was the largest church west of Chicago.

THE STOCKADE REFUGE is flanked by *Perry Street,* one of only three or four authentic cobblestone streets left in America. The stockade was built during the Black Hawk War at a time when fears of Indian uprisings could send many thousands of area farmers, miners and families fleeing to Galena for shelter. Indian artifacts are exhibited and some of the original stockade has been excavated. Small fee.

LOLLY'S DOLL AND TOY MUSEUM is located on 225 Magazine St. It is a personal collection of more than 1000 dolls and dollhouse accessories.

THE GALENA PIONEER CEMETERY is located on Washington Street, just behind *Grant's first home* at 121 High Street. The cemetery contains the graves of the area's earliest settlers and miners. Some graves date from before 1812 and contain remains brought west by people who made homes in Galena. Many of the miners from Cornwall are buried here. The land was donated by a Capt. Gear who came to the Galena lead diggings without a penny to his name. Eventually he discovered a lode on Tower Hill from which he took 26,000,000 pounds of ore. Lead ore at the time was selling for $80 a ton. . . .

SPECIAL EVENTS

Early JUNE   *Spring Tour of Homes.*
Skills from the Hills. Traditional Arts and Crafts Displays.

Mid-JUNE   *Annual Galena Art Festival* at the Old Market Historic Site. Juried Art Fair with more than 50 booths.

4th of JULY   *Old Fashioned 4th of July*, Flea Market Antique Town Rod Run.

Late SEPTEMBER   *Fall Tour of Homes.*

3rd weekend in OCTOBER   Amtrak trains come in from Chicago. *Fall color tours*, art/craft displays.

Early OCTOBER   *U.S. Grant Antique Market.* Dealers from throughout the midwest gather under one roof.

FOR A COMPLETE LODGING DIRECTORY, OR FURTHER INFORMATION ON WHAT TO SEE OR DO CONTACT : The Galena/Jo Daviess County Convention and Visitors Bureau, 101 Bouthillier Street, Galena, IL. 61036 or call toll free (800) 747-9377. Call the Dubuque Convention and Visitors Bureau toll free at (800) 79-VISIT.

Galena seen from Grant Park

STEAMBOAT'S COMIN'!

It was the introduction of Robert Fulton's steamboat, the *Clermont,* in 1807, that changed the course of commercial history on the Mississippi. First used in New Orleans in 1811, it is believed that more than 1100 steamboats were ferrying trade up and down the river by the mid-1800's.

River traffic before the wood and coal burning steamboats became widely used was largely a one-way affair. While canoes and eventually flat-bottomed boats could carry some passengers and such freight as fur, lead, salt, and agricultural goods down river, it took sheer muscle power to get a freight-laden boat back up river. Many of the larger flat-bottomed boats were simply broken up and sold for scrap. The crews would then hike back up river to bring down another boat.

In 1823, however, the Army proved that the Upper Mississippi was deep enough for steamboat traffic all the way to Fort Snelling, near St. Paul, MN. Lead ore from the southwestern corner of the Wisconsin Territory and other products from the Upper Mississippi could now be transported in profitable quantities.

Many of the earliest settlers on the upper reaches of the river stockpiled cordwood for cash as the boats gradually pushed north. The steamboats were burning 30 to 40 cords a day, for which they paid $2.50 each. Often, the steamboats were loaded from service boats so that the big vessels never had to stop.

During the 1850's, immigrants began pouring into the

country, often to the river terminals at St. Louis. The steamboats began ferrying passengers in great boat loads to the north. The riverboat became the life blood of mid-America and the daring river pilots were the heroes of the day. During their brief reign, great wooden sternwheelers and sidewheelers provided the most dependable transportation available on the river.

In the 1880's the railroads began forging their way through bush, bluff and backwater swamps to claim a share of this bonanza of freight and passenger business. The railroads instituted vicious rate wars; and easier access to the rails meant that, gradually, the shipment of goods and passenger services switched from steamboat to rail.

The railroad, once built, did not have to contend with fog, snags or low water and offered service right through the winter. Settlements once isolated by unnavigable waters now found themselves booming as railroads provided overland transportation.

Riverboat traffic dwindled. Towns like Galena, IL, which had staked their commercial futures on the steamboats, were passed by.

Since WWI, modern-day towboats and barges have taken the place of the steamboat. One powerful towboat can push as many as 15 fully-laden barges of grain, coal and other freight. Such a load moves the tonnage of five or six freight trains at considerably less expense.

The only true floating palaces still providing overnight excursion services along the Upper Mississippi River are the *Delta Queen* and the *Mississippi Queen*. What a treat it is is to meet one unexpectedly or to see its lights and hear the merry calliope pumping far across the river in the dark.

Several river towns now provide smaller excursion boats. *Robert's River Rides* offers an 11-hour trip from Dubuque to Bettendorf, IA, and there is one three-day trip (on the *Viking* cruiser) operating between St. Paul, MN, and La Crosse, WI.

The popular excursion steamer, the J.S., pictured in the late 1800's.

APPENDIX

CREDITS

Ceramic Pot sketch by Ronda Ulrath, Mississippi Valley
    Archaeological Center. p. 88

Paintings by Marion Biehn. Used with permission of the State Bank
    of La Crosse. pp. 30, 84, 164

Photos from the Upper Mississippi River National Wildlife and Fish
    Refuge, Winona office. pp. 40, 10, 34, 52, 49, 106, 125, 138,
    207

Photos by Pat Middleton. pp. 108, 125, 174, 190, 196

Photo by Rich Mettille, Holmen. p. 4

Photo and Fur Trader sketch by Julie Sheppard. pp. 92, 180

Photos courtesy of the Area Research Center, UW-L. pp. 59, 154

Black River information from the Wisconsin D.N.R. p. 80

Galena City Map from the Galena/Jo Daviess County Historical
    Society. p. 193

Brief History, p. 203, adapted from 1964 Wisconsin State Blue Book.

Port of Potosi Special Feature courtesy of the Potosi/Tennyson
    Historical Society. p. 175

History of Genoa based on original research of Nancy Jambois
    (History of Genoa) and David Venner.

A BRIEF HISTORY OF THE UPPER MISSISSIPPI

Under the French Flag

1634	Jean Nicolet reaches Wisconsin via Lake Michigan in search of the Northwest Passage.
1654-56	Radisson and Groseillier are first official emissaries of the fur trade.
1666	Nicholas Perrot opens fur trade with area Indians.
1673	Jolliet and Marquette discover the Mississippi from the mouth of the Wisconsin River.
1678	Duluth, Hennepin and Pepin explore the northern reaches of the Mississippi and the western end of Lake Superior, so called because it was the furthest north of the Great Lakes.
1690	Perrot discovers Indian lead mines in Wisconsin and Iowa.
1763	The Treaty of Paris. The upper Mississippi River valley becomes a British Colony.

Under the Spanish Flag

1541	DeSoto is the first European to explore the southern reaches of the Mississippi. The Louisiana Territory eventually stretches north as far as McGregor, IA.
1790	Julien Dubuque begins working his lead mines under license from Spain.

Brief History, continued

Under the English Flag

1766   Jonathan Carver explores the Mississippi seeking a Northwest Passage.

1774   Quebec Act makes Upper Mississippi a part of the province of Quebec, one cause of the American revolution.

1781   Settlement at Prairie du Chien.

1783   Upper Mississippi becomes part of the United States.

Under the American Flag

1804   Harrison's treaty with Indians at St. Louis extinguishes Indian title to the lead region, a cause of the Black Hawk War.

1815   The War of 1812 ends, and with it, British rule in the Upper Mississippi. In 1816 Fort Crawford is built on the site of the British Fort Shelby and Astor's American Fur Co. begins operations.

1822   Mining leases begin in Wisconsin territory.

1823   The steamer *Virginia* follows the Mississippi north from St. Louis to Fort Snelling proving that the river can be traversed the entire length.

1832   Black Hawk War ends at Victory, WI, in Battle of Bad Ax.

1848   Wisconsin becomes a state under Pres. James Polk.

1857   Railroad is completed to Prairie du Chien.

1860   Wisconsin presidential vote goes to Abraham Lincoln.

1861   Civil War begins.

1894   Spanish American War.

Where to LOOK for the Birds

The UPPER MISSISSIPPI NATIONAL WILDLIFE AND FISH REFUGE was designated in 1924, well before the lock & dam system was developed for commercial shipping. As a result, we have a national wildlife treasure in relatively untouched river bottoms — a mecca for birds. Fred Lesher, a dedicated area birder, offers here some suggestions on where birds *may* be found along the Upper Mississippi.

The TREMPEALEAU WILDLIFE REFUGE is an excellent stop. Ospreys and double-crested cormorants nest here. Eagles in winter, spring. Many other species may be seen.

The EAGLE VALLEY NATURE PRESERVE just west of Cassville for eagle and hawk watching.

Concentrations of winter eagles at BLACKHAWK PARK near Victory, WI. Nests visible February-March from Minnesota side along Hwy 26 in Houston County.

Bald eagles will be seen soaring over the bluff sides along the Great River Road in early spring. They are solitary birds with wings out flat. The turkey vulture is nearly as large, but soars in pairs or large groups called "kettles." Wing profile of the vultures is a distinct "V" shape.

Watch for bald eagles during spring/fall migration at O.L. KIPP State Park in Minnesota. Also WYALUSING State Park near Prairie du Chien and NELSON DEWEY State Park near Cassville. McGregor and Guttenburg, IA, for wintering eagles above and below dams, where water remains open. Eagles become more abundant to the south because of milder conditions. Great numbers of wintering eagles at Davenport, IA., Rock Island, IL, and Clinton, IA - Lock & Dam numbers 13, 14, and 15.

Cerulean warblers, Acadian flycatchers and Louisiana waterthrush nest at BEAVER CREEK VALLEY State Park near Caledonia, MN. Kentucky warblers nest at WYALUSING State Park, WI. Turkeys may be found on hillsides in the Genoa-Stoddard area, the YELLOW RIVER State Forest near Harpers Ferry, IA, and Hwy 249 between Reno and Caledonia, MN.

A special Butterfly Garden is located at BELLEVUE, IA, State Park. Special plantings to attract butterflies. Excellent river views and birding at EFFIGY MOUNDS NATIONAL MONU-MENT in Iowa and at EAGLE POINT Parks in both Clinton and Dubuque, IA.

Whistling swans have been renamed tundra swans. Tundra swans migrate up river in early April and are identified in the field by straight, upright necks. At times, there may be 15,000 swans in open water between Genoa, WI, and Wabasha, MN. Rare trumpeter swans are being introduced into the Twin Cities in Minnesota.

Peregrine falcons nest at Alma across from the power generating plants and at JOHN LATSCH State Park just north of Winona. The peregrine falcon is between the size of a kestrel and a red-tailed hawk. A big falcon, with sideburns. Very fast flier.

Prothonotary warblers on Shore Acres Road, along *STH 14 & 61* between La Crosse and La Crescent, and south of the pool 7 dike on French Island in La Crosse.

"I have been observing the warbler migration in La Crosse for 21 years and I feel that during the last 5 or 6 years the numbers of individual birds and varieties of species returning in the spring from Central and South America have dramatically dwindled. The numbers are way down, perhaps due to habitat lost as the rain forests in Central and South America are decimated.

On the other hand, the river may be cleaner and river wildlife and nesting birds appear more abundant. These changes may be part of larger cycles, however, rather than the immediate result of any changes in river quality or habitat loss."

Fred Lesher

An effort is being made to reestablish the Peregrin falcon in the Mississippi River Valley.

Do you need information on lodging, attractions, or local events? Listed here are many organizations which will be more than happy to help.

STATE Departments of Tourism

Wisconsin: Please call 1-800-ESCAPES or FAX 608-266-3403
Minnesota: 1-800-652-9747 (in MN) or 1-800-657-3700 (Nat'l) FAX 612-296-7095
Iowa: Travel & Tourism Division, 600 East Court St., Des Moines, IA 50309 FAX 515-281-7276
Illinois: Bureau of Tourism, 620 E. Adams, Springfield, IL 62701 217-785-6352 or FAX 217-785-6454

REGIONAL Tourism Agencies

Eastern Iowa Tourism Assoc.
P.O. Box 178, S. Downey St.
West Branch, IA 52358
1-319-643-2848
1-800-348-1837

Mississippi River Parkway Comm.
Suite 1513
336 Robert Street
St. Paul, MN 55101
PHONE 612-224-9903
FAX 612-297-6896

Galena/Jo Daviess County Convention & Visitors Bureau
101 Bouthillier Street
Galena, IL 61036
1-800-747-9377

Hidden Valleys (Representing nine counties of Southwestern WI)
P.O. Box 5, 6711 Settlement Rd
Cassville, WI 53806
1-608-725-5867

Wisconsin Indian Head Country (for areas north of La Crosse)
Box 628
Chetek, WI 54728
715-834-2781
1-800-472-6654 (WI)
1-800-826-6966 (surrounding states)

County and Local Contacts

Allamakee County
David A. Wilson
PO Box 359
Lansing, IA 52151

Buffalo County Clerk's Office
Courthouse Annex
Alma, WI 54610
608-685-4940

Clayton County
Mary Fitch
Rt. 1, Box 239
Spook Cave
McGregor, IA 52157
319-873-2144

Crawford County
UWEX Office
111 W. Dunn
Prairie du Chien, W. 53821
608-326-6431

Dubuque Convention & Visitors
Bureau
770 Town Clock Plaza
Dubuque, IA 52001
319-557-9200
800-79-VISIT

Fountain City Clerk
City Hall
Fountain City, WI 54629

Grant County
UWEX Office
PO Box 31
Lancaster, WI 53813
608-723-2125

Nelson Village Clerk
RR 1, PO Box 12
Nelson, WI 54726

Pepin County
Court House
PO Box 39
Durand, WI 54736
715-672-5214

Pierce County
UWEX Office
414 W. Main Street
Ellsworth, WI 54011
715-273-3531, ext 243

Trempealeau County
County Clerk's Office
Whitehall, WI 54773
715-538-2311

Vernon County UWEX Office
PO Box 392
Viroqua, WI 54665

Village of Trempealeau
Village Clerk
Trempealeau, WI 54661

Viroqua Chamber of Commerce
Viroqua, W. 54665

LOCAL Chambers of Commerce

Alma City Clerk's Office
Box 277
Alma, WI 54610
608-685-3330

Cassville Civic Club
Box 576
Cassville, WI 53806

Dodgeville Chamber of Commerce
N. Bequette St
Dodgeville, WI 53533
608-935-5993

La Crosse Convention & Visitors Bureau
Riverside Park
P.O. Box 1895
La Crosse, WI 54602-1895
608-782-2366

Potosi-Tennyson Chamber of Commerce
97 E. Main St.
Potosi-Tennyson, WI 53820
608-763-2221

Prairie du Chien Chamber of Commerce
211 S. Main St.
P.O. Box 326
Prairie du Chien, WI 53821
608-326-8555

Prescott Chamber of Commerce
P.O. Box 244
Prescott, WI 54021

Syttende Mai, Inc.
P.O. Box 31
Westby, WI 54667

Lake City Chamber
212 S. Washington St.
Lake City, MN 55041
(612) 345-4123

Red Wing Chamber
P.O. Box 133
Red Wing, MN 55066
(612) 388-4719

Wabasha Chamber
Attn: Shirley Behrns
City Hall
Wabasha, MN 55981

Winona Visitor's Bureau
Winona, MN 55987
(507) 452-2272